I0445327

MANAGING
— YOUR —
HABITS
FOR
SUCCESS

DANNY ZELAYA

Managing Your Habits for Success: How to Improve at Work and in Life by Paying Attention to Your Habits
Copyright © 2022 Danny Zelaya

Published by Danny Zelaya

Hardcover ISBN: 979-8-9869816-0-4
Ebook ISBN: 979-8-9869816-1-1
Paperback ISBN: 979-8-9869816-2-8
Library of Congress: 2022920055

Printed in the United States

To my parents—immigrants who came to America seeking a better life. My success is because of you.

CONTENTS

PART II
DEVELOPING NEW HABITS

WHY I WROTE THIS BOOK
AND HOW TO READ IT

On a Monday morning, I began my workday as usual. I logged into my computer—and typed my password incorrectly. Frustrated, I typed my password again— only faster this time! I mistyped it again. Fearing getting locked out and ruining half my day, I slowed down and retyped my password carefully. I pressed "enter" and anxiously waited for the result. It worked! Once logged in, I opened the same folders, documents, and spreadsheets in the same order. I began working on my inbox by replying to emails, searching for messages, moving emails around, and deleting many of them. I skimmed most of the emails without thoroughly reading any of them. I had new tasks to complete, messages to follow up on, and ongoing work from the previous week to begin. I had meetings and activities scheduled into my calendar that were beginning to appear on the screen as reminders. As I began to work, I noticed I was following the same pattern as last Monday . . . and the Monday before that . . . and the Monday previous to that. I began the workday and workweek in the same way without thinking about it. I did the same things.

And everything felt the same. I had the same results, and I was in the same place as the previous year. Time had moved forward, but I had not. I had not grown or improved.

At home, I began to notice the same repeating patterns as well. I noticed I visited the same stores and drove the same routes. I regularly visited the same places, and I rarely ever visited a new place. In conversations with my wife, we talked about the same things and responded to the same triggers in the same way. The behavioral responses were predictable at work and at home. There were many things I repeatedly did in the same situations. But most of what I repeatedly did I was not aware of.

I did it automatically, and it felt normal.

Things started to change when I began to pay attention to the moments when my habits arose. In those moments, I asked myself, "Can this be improved?" If what I was inclined to do could be improved, I wrote it down. If a task, project, activity, habit, or meeting could be improved, I wrote it down. I then implemented the improvement, and growth slowly happened.

One principle we learn early in life while attending school is to pay attention. Our teachers constantly tell us to pay attention. We gain knowledge by being attentive and interested in things. In this book, the same principle is applied to learning about yourself. If you pay attention to your habits, you can improve them. You want to re-evaluate your habits to see if they're good for you. If not, you can change them.

I wrote this book for leaders at all levels wishing to improve their results. But the principles can be applied to anyone wanting to improve at work and in life. The book is divided into two parts for two specific reasons. The first part of the book focuses on your existing habits and how to change them. You must first become aware of your habits and then make the decision to improve. We examine the role of your thoughts, beliefs, and surrounding environment because they're influential in the formation and continuation of your habits. Part I comprises the majority of the content. Take your time going through each chapter in Part I. The information is vital to changing your outlook on life and mastering your habits. In Part II, we shift the focus to how we can develop and stay consistent with new habits. There is only one chapter in Part II, and the writing style is direct. I designed this chapter so you can quickly get to work on building new habits. It's also designed for you to continually come back to the chapter as a reference guide. If you wish to get a head start on developing new habits, you can go straight to Part II.

But a word of caution. Many of the habits you want to have are influenced by your existing habits. Without being aware of your existing habits and working to change them, you may find it difficult to develop new habits.

As you read each chapter, you will likely have ideas, thoughts, and questions that arise. Write them down in the notes section at the end of each chapter. Once you review your notes, if you find something useful to apply, do something about it. Make the decision to change and get on with the work of improving.

If you're interested in becoming a better leader, you must become what you want to be. By improving your habits, tomorrow becomes better than today.

WHAT DOES IT MEAN TO MANAGE YOURSELF?

Monday morning. It's still dark outside, but James has already had his first cup of coffee, showered, checked his calendar for today's meetings, and scanned his emails for more fires to put out and for an update on the project his team is overseeing. *How is it possible he is already behind?* It's already a long day, and the day hasn't even started yet. His wife, Mary, has an early budget meeting, so he rushes to drop the kids off at their school and beat the traffic to his office before back-to-back morning video conference meetings begin. James swings by the office kitchen to grab a cup of coffee, returns the greetings of a few on his team, then heads to his desk to host the first morning video conference. He's finished several meetings with no break in between and begins reading and answering new emails while catching up with previous ones. He visits with his colleagues in the office and then quickly grabs lunch to eat on the run as he checks on local projects in the field. By the time he's done with field visits, he's behind again on the dozens of new emails that have come in.

***

The life of a leader is hectic. You have early morning meetings, hour-by-hour meetings, endless emails, rapidly changing initiatives, staffing challenges, frequent field visits, a full travel schedule, and recurring business reviews. If you lead a small business, life can feel just as hectic. You have fewer resources, and you complete more tasks with little to no help from others. You may also have your own personal goals to achieve but struggle with your own personal growth.

While you're leading others, how do you manage and lead *yourself* for success?

Answering that important question is the focus of this book, and part of discovering the answer is looking within.

While the focus is always outside of yourself when leading others, in managing yourself, the focus is on *you*. You rely on your knowledge, skills, and work ethic to effectively lead your team and business to success. But just as your team and business need to grow, *you* also need to grow. You *can* improve and *must* improve to realize your potential, meet the changing needs of the times, and lead effectively into the future.

When you manage yourself, instead of thinking about what the business or team needs to improve, the focus shifts to what you can do to improve. This attention to personal development can have a tremendously positive effect on your well-being, your relationship with others, and the success of your team and business.

Being a leader can be a very lonely position. The more

leadership responsibilities you have, the fewer people with your responsibilities are available who you can talk to, relate with, and receive encouragement from. The position of leadership can make you feel lonely even while surrounded by people.

The good news is you can manage yourself for success regardless of your circumstances. You can feel forgotten and ignored—and still manage yourself for success. You can feel alone—and still manage yourself for success. You can feel like you're drowning in work—and still manage yourself for success. *Whatever your circumstances, you can manage yourself for success.*

Managing yourself means taking greater responsibility to improve and achieve your goals. It means appreciating your uniqueness and ability to improve. You take responsibility for your attitude, the goals you want to achieve, and the habits you want to have. Your attitude sets the direction for how you relate with others, experience the world, and how you see yourself. Your beliefs inform your attitude, but it's your attitude that leads the way.

Consider the way a ship sails the open sea. The captain navigates from the bridge and gives directions for the sailors to follow. If you think of yourself as a ship, your beliefs and thoughts are the navigation bridge that provides you with direction. Your attitude is the forward part of the ship, and it leads the way.

Before you can take responsibility for yourself to improve, you must *want* it. Change only happens when you desire it and make it happen. You must lead with the attitude that you're going to learn from yourself and from the situations you're in. You're going to learn from life, and every day is a learning opportunity. Without an attitude of learning, you will not learn and grow.

Once you've taken responsibility for your attitude of learning, set your mind on the goals you want to achieve. Goals are important in improving and changing your habits. You can have various goals in life, such as career, finance, education, travel, family, relationship, leadership, spiritual, exercise, time management, sleep, and reading goals. Your goals reflect what's important to you. Taking responsibility for your goals means having clarity about what you want to achieve. Define the goals you want to achieve as clearly as possible. This is often difficult because of the time and attention needed to think about what you want. In our digital world, it's easy to get distracted, and it's becoming harder to spend time thinking about what's important to you. Goals require considerable effort and attention, but only you can determine them, and only you can achieve them.

To achieve your goals, pay attention to your habits. Habits are the things you repeatedly do in familiar moments. Habits are very powerful because they're consistent, ingrained within you, and often go unnoticed. Your habits bring you closer to or further from achieving your goals. For the purpose of this book, we will focus on understanding, identifying, and transforming your habits. If you know what you repeatedly do, you can have more control over what you *want* to do.

Habits are learned, and they become instinctive and feel natural. This is where the benefits and disadvantages of habits come in. If your habits are good and desirable, they help you achieve your goals. For example, putting on your seat belt in a car is a regularly repeated action, and that repetition helps keep you safe. The consistent repetition of habits helps you achieve your goals. But sometimes, the outcome of your habits hinders the goals you want to achieve. If you're bored in a meeting, and you habitually pick up your phone to scroll for information as a distraction, this habit prevents you from being attentive to the meeting, and this can create an impression that you're disinterested in the topic and the people within the meeting. Although your habit of picking up your phone when bored gives you the desired distraction, it can also hinder your goal of contributing your best ideas to the meeting.

A strong focus in this book is on your habits of *thought*, which are your mental habits. All of your habits begin in your mind. Your mental habits are your repeating thoughts and beliefs that arise in response to a familiar situation. You know them by what you frequently and automatically tell yourself. For example, when an opportunity arises for you to advance in your career, take a risk on a project, or contribute your ideas in a meeting, do you become fearful and doubt yourself? Someone once told you that you don't have the charisma to succeed, and you believed them. As a result, you falsely believe you can't be a good leader. You now habitually withdraw from leadership opportunities because of what you automatically tell yourself when a leadership opportunity arises. You're afraid to raise your hand because of what you incorrectly tell yourself. You have a mental habit that repeats the same negative thoughts and beliefs as if they're true, even though they happen to be false. The truth is you can, in fact, be a good leader. Your habits are driven by your thoughts and beliefs, but your mental process is so quick that it's hard to notice the specific thoughts that motivate your habits.

Your habitual behavior is what you typically see. These are your physical actions. Since your thoughts are invisible, your habits are visible through your behavior. Your behavior is significant because it *reveals* what you're thinking. Your behavior can reveal your habitual thoughts and beliefs. There are moments when you seem to always behave and respond in the same way and do the same thing. You have behavioral patterns you repeat regularly.

Many of our habits are so ingrained within us that we're not aware of them. They feel normal. We've learned to live with them, and we repeat them without observing if they're good for us. We do many activities not because we think it's the best way to achieve what we want but because it's what we are accustomed to and comfortable with.

One assumption I make in this book is that your habits are mainly good. You've developed them to achieve *something*. They serve a purpose for you. If you've managed to achieve many of your most important goals—in your education, family, personal relationships, career, and personal projects—your habits have helped you achieve them. If you have new goals you want to achieve, your habits will also help you achieve them.

Success is a gradual process. You may have achieved success in many things, but to improve and achieve greater success, you need to pay attention to your habits and take responsibility for them. If you can adjust the habits that need improvement, you will find greater success.

How do you take responsibility for your habits?

Managing yourself for success begins by paying attention to your habits. You're simply being more observant by being self-aware.

Self-awareness is an attitude of learning about yourself. We pay more attention to the behavior of others than to our own behavior, but we can learn a lot about ourselves if we are self-aware of our habits. Unfortunately, we often pay attention to the wrong things. We don't pay attention to what's true and, instead, believe what's not true about ourselves.

As you grow in self-awareness, you'll notice that your habits are significantly influenced by certain areas of your life, such as your environment and beliefs. Your environment includes your upbringing, the groups you belong to, and the culture or physical surroundings in which you live. To grow, you must be willing to let go of certain beliefs that were previously helpful to you but are no longer helpful in your development.

It's a common desire to want more control over your career and life. You can feel stuck in life and not realize that your habits are often what prevent you from advancing forward. The main idea to take from this book is you can improve at anything by paying attention to your habits. You can manage yourself to improve by taking responsibility for your habits. You can manage yourself for success.

This journey is not easy, but it is worthwhile. Paying attention to your habits is difficult in a digital world with constant distractions and notifications, but with a little patience and consistency in developing your self awareness, you can have greater success. You will see the improvements, experience the satisfaction of achievement, and grow in excitement for each new positive habit you develop along the way.

By paying attention and taking responsibility for your habits, you can improve at virtually anything. You can manage yourself to improve and achieve your goals. You can manage yourself for success, no matter what leadership position you have. If you're a CEO, executive, middle manager, small business owner, entrepreneur, professional, office manager, religious leader, employee, or someone who just wants to become a better leader, you can manage yourself to improve, accomplish your goals, and achieve greater success.

Managing yourself for success begins and ends with taking greater responsibility to improve.

Let's do this together. Are you ready to begin?

PART

I

AWARENESS OF YOUR HABITS

CHAPTER 1

BELIEFS

Your Beliefs Support Your Habits.

I n his free time, James likes to exercise. With his music playlist and workout routine ready, he's a workout machine. He occasionally flexes in the mirror and likes the pump he sees. He feels good after he exercises, and one of his goals is to exercise more often. One hot weekend, his friend Robert texts him to ask if he's free to help him move to a new two-story house. James owns a pickup truck, and he's very popular when his friends need something moved. He thinks of the idea of moving furniture and carrying boxes up the two-story house, and although he will be exercising—which he enjoys—he suddenly doesn't seem so enthusiastic about exercising. The thought of sweating now sucks. He'd rather sweat and lift weights at the gym—not sweat and lift boxes. Lifting heavier weights at the gym is a sign of progress and pride, but the thought of lifting a couch and furniture is tiring. James agrees to help, but before he replies, Robert sends a text saying he has enough people to help him, and James's help isn't needed anymore. James is relieved and replies by saying, "OK, no problem! Let me know if you need help later!" Relieved, he is even more motivated to go to the gym.

Although James was going to exercise by helping Robert move, what he *believes* about going to the gym and helping his friend move influences how he feels and what he does. Your beliefs influence your thoughts and actions.

Your Beliefs Influence What You Think and Do

What you think and do affects the direction of your day and life. If you recall our metaphor of the ship in the introduction, your beliefs are the navigation deck of a ship. They help direct your course. Your beliefs give you direction based on what you believe to be true or false about yourself, the world, and others. Your beliefs affect your attitude, behavior, and virtually everything about you. It is, therefore, important to pay attention to your beliefs and how they influence your thoughts and daily direction.

Your thoughts consist of ideas, self-dialogue (self-talk), and beliefs (statements you believe are true). Thoughts are what you say to yourself about things. Many are random and just float away, but others tend to stick with you and frequently reappear. Some of your thoughts express and reveal what you believe. You may express your thoughts out loud, such as when people say, "I think out loud," or "I have a big mouth," or your thoughts may play internally and stay unshared. Even if you don't express your thoughts, they can be loud in your head.

You have thoughts about yourself, others, and the world. You're familiar with your thoughts but not as familiar with your beliefs. Behind many of your thoughts are your beliefs, and it's your beliefs that motivate many of your thoughts. Your thoughts can be random, but your beliefs are always specific.

What's a Belief?

You have beliefs—ideas you hold to be true—about yourself, others, and the world. Beliefs are what you affirm is true about reality. When you think of reality, you largely think of yourself, others, and the world you live in, and you have beliefs about all three. Your beliefs develop when your mind organizes events, information, and experiences into ideas that you accept as real or true.

What you believe to be true is not always personally verified. You can be in love with Paris without ever having visited the city. You can also have thoughts *without* actually believing in them, such as when you talk about imaginary creatures like dragons as if they were real. We don't believe in their existence, but we do think about them as if they are real. We imagine worlds where they exist and include them in movies, art, books, and fictional stories. You can also have thoughts that you believe are true but are *not* true to reality; we call these *false beliefs*. Prejudice is a common form of false belief, as it spreads negative ideas about others that are not personally verified, not based on personal experience, or not true of everyone in a given group. The way you tend to think and often *what* you tend to think are influenced by your beliefs. Your beliefs are the key to many of your thoughts, and they set the tone for what you think and how you think each day.

You have an emotional connection to many of your beliefs. You feel some beliefs very strongly—such as political, religious, moral, and leadership beliefs. Beliefs that have to do with your upbringing also have a strong emotional connection because they form the basis of your identity. Many of your beliefs form the basis of your values, which are your strongest beliefs about how life should work.

There are some beliefs you feel strongly and some less strongly. There are some beliefs you outgrow and discard in time and some you hold firmly from your upbringing. And there are some beliefs you develop the more you experience and interact with life.

How Do You Acquire Your Beliefs?

You acquire your beliefs through the ideas and information you receive from your environment. People are your most influential environment. They are part of your social circles, groups you belong to, and workplace. Your home and family are environments. Your upbringing is part of your environment, with unique people, expectations, and culture that shaped who you are today. You grew up in a group environment, and you continue to live and work within a group environment. You're constantly interacting with your group environment and receiving information and ideas from that interaction. For example, if your primary source of information about people and the world is from social media, your favorite media channel, media personality, or group-membership magazine, the information you receive is filtered to support their interests and, consequently, your beliefs may be skewed toward a particular perspective. You form your beliefs by the information and ideas you receive from interacting with people, the world, and what you tell yourself.

You're always learning from others. Since you can't personally experience everything or have knowledge of everything, you trust what others say. When you receive ideas and information from people, you begin to form beliefs about what they say. Your group environment plays a strong role in forming your beliefs because of the ideas and information you receive from them.

Beliefs Provide a Repetition to Life

Your beliefs and values provide you with a feeling of security, and they give direction to your life. Values provide people with standards and expectations of behavior. Your values and beliefs tell you that if you do what's expected in life and in your career, life will play out fairly in the way it's supposed to. For example, if you believe working hard leads to a favorable outcome, like being promoted, you will continue to work hard because you believe the results of your hard work will lead to where you want to go. You believe your actions will lead to your desired outcome. You, therefore, believe you have some control of your life and destiny.

You also trust there's a daily order of events that happen, a repetition to life that you rely on. When you go to bed, you

5

believe the next day will begin when you wake up. You get out of bed, get ready, go to work, and continue achieving your goals. There's a repetition to life that you believe in and depend on. Repetition is important to achieving your goals. You believe one thing leads to another because that is what you learn and observe.

You repeat many things because you have expectations. Expectations form from what you believe. You have expectations for today, tomorrow, and next week. You believe life is supposed to move in orderly stages with an expected progression of time moving forward. Based on that belief, you often ask yourself and others, "What's next?" Think of how many times you've asked someone, "What's next in your career? What do you want to do after this?" Or you may ask yourself, "What's the next phase in life for me? What position or job do I want next?" If you receive a promotion or take a new job, it's common to post on your social media: "Grateful for this new opportunity in life" or "Grateful for this new chapter in my life."

The following are some examples of common thoughts and expectations we tend to believe:

- If I work hard, I'll get a promotion and raise.
- If I get a promotion, I'll have more money to do things.
- I'm next in line for a promotion.
- The job I want will always be there.
- If my kids graduate from college, they will have a good job waiting for them.

- If I get a degree, my income will be higher than not getting a degree.
- If I spend all my hours working, my spouse and family will still be there for me.
- If I work a certain number of years, I will have a good retirement.
- My job will exist until my retirement years.
- When I retire, I'll have the health and energy to travel.
- When I retire, I'll have more time for my personal goals.
- I'll always have the income to pay for my growing expenses.
- Next year will be better than this year.
- The future will be better than today.
- Tomorrow I'll have more time than today.
- My customers will always choose my business.
- My donating members will always choose my organization.
- I'll spend time with the people closest to me later in life.

All the beliefs above can be true, but they are not *guaranteed* to be true. You act on these beliefs because you expect the desired outcome. Many of your beliefs about life and the future assume a cause-and-effect relationship.

You see the world and interpret the events around you through a cause-and-effect outlook because you like to give order, meaning, and certainty to events. You like to know the reasons for things because it gives you a sense of more control in life.

To know the reason for something is to know the cause, and if you know the cause, you can control the desired outcome. This helps you make decisions by believing that what you do will lead to the outcome you desire. You do one thing, or a series of things, in order to get what you want. You also do things to avoid what you don't want or are uncomfortable with. Procrastinating, for example, is something you do to avoid an activity you don't want to do. Your beliefs provide a repetition to life, and they give you consistent direction on what to do, what to expect, and how to respond to life's moments.

The Beginning of Your Habits

From what you observe in life, you learn that one thing can lead to another. From these observations, you start making predictions about what *should* happen. Once you see that something you've experienced before arises again, you can repeat what you did the last time. This is the beginning of your habits. A moment happens, and you do something, and when that moment happens again, you repeat what you did before to achieve the same outcome. Your habits form by *knowing* that one thing leads to another.

Habits are great because they're easy to repeat, but that is also their weakness. One thing leads to another, and you start assuming that association should *always* happen. Something happened one time, and you then believe it should happen every time that moment arises again.

Your beliefs provide you with a repetition to life, and they give you direction in life. But you must also be willing to pay attention to life *as it is* to both challenge your beliefs and develop more accurate beliefs. You must be willing to pay attention to the present moment.

Your Beliefs Support Your Habits

On a trip to San Francisco, I wore my dark blue business suit with a vest. My shirt was white, with dark blue dress pants, vest, and coat. While boarding the plane, I used the restroom in the back (I hate using the restroom while in flight). When I was done, I started walking toward the front of the plane. As I was walking to my seat, a woman asked me to help her with her luggage. I gladly helped pick up her heavy luggage (not sure what she had in there!) and placed it inside the bin. She thanked me and asked me if I sold pretzels. *Pretzels*? "Uh, no," I answered but told her someone in the back probably did.

After helping her, I continued toward the front. A person who was seated stood up and asked me if I had crackers. *Crackers*?! I told her I didn't have crackers, but I did have a protein bar that was mine. She asked me if I had any other food, and I said, "No, sorry," while walking away from her.

Right before I got to my seat, another woman asked me to help her with her bags. I finally figured out what was going on but still proceeded to help her with the bags anyway. Another person looked at me, and I knew what they were going to ask me. I quickly said, "I'm not a flight attendant. I know I have a vest on, but I'm not a flight attendant. Sorry." And I sat down as quickly as I could. I did not use the restroom or get up for the rest of the flight.

I no longer wear a suit with a vest anymore on a plane.

How did many people incorrectly believe I was a flight attendant? They assumed one thing always leads to another. There are many flight attendants who wear dark blue dress pants, white shirts, dark blue vests, and sometimes a coat. But they tend to have colored stripes on their coats or vests, a name tag, colored ties, and wings that are pinned to their vests or coats. I had none of those uniform traits, but people assumed that when someone wore what I wore, it meant they were a flight attendant. Why? Because that's what they knew to be true from experience, but they did not pay attention to the fact that what I was wearing was *different*. They saw something, my clothes, and they had the same idea they'd had in the past: people who wear my clothes are flight attendants. They acted on what they learned to be true in the past and repeated that response in the present. But the present moment was unique and different.

How you perceive something influences your actions. What you believe about something influences what you do. What you believe to be true you do.

Your habits form because of what you believe about a particular moment and what to do in that moment. Your beliefs link a situation and an action together. Your beliefs bond them together. There is a pattern to your habits.

Examples of Beliefs Leading to Habits

Belief	Habit
"Buckling my seat belt keeps me safe."	Using your seat belt every time
"This is the only way to express my intense feelings."	Swearing
"Leaders speak the same language."	Communicating in group jargon
"I don't have time to eat healthy."	Grabbing a fast-food lunch
"I need to be accessible 24/7."	Checking email inbox every few minutes

Your beliefs support your habits. When you pick up your mobile phone habitually, for example, you reach for it because you believe that picking it up will fulfill the urge that prompted you, i.e., the news, social media, or email inbox. The habit of picking up your phone is so familiar that you're not aware of how often you do it. But you do it for a reason. You know that habit leads to a desired outcome. If, however, you remove the social media app, you will still feel prompted to check your phone for social media until your mind recognizes that checking your phone cannot satisfy your desire. You begin to believe that checking your phone for social media isn't possible, and your habit changes. You react in a certain way because you *believe* a certain way. Your habits are supported by your beliefs, and what you believe about something is how you respond to it.

On many occasions, I've called out to someone in a crowd I thought I knew but who simply had a resemblance to the person I know. While at a gas station recently, as I latched the fuel pump nozzle into my car's fuel tank, I noticed a person in another lane loudly say, "Hey, Jimmy!" The person he was calling had his back toward him on the opposite side of the lane, and he didn't reply. The man again said, "Hey, Jimmy!" When the person he called turned around, both looked at each other, and the person who called out started laughing and said he was sorry. Both knew it was a mistaken identity and laughed at the event.

We can misjudge situations subconsciously, and this is what can happen with our habits, as we develop habits in response to situations—even when the situations are not real or true. This can lead you to do something habitually based on false information. If you're snorkeling and believe the shadows in the water created by the clouds overhead are actually sharks, you'll begin to panic, and the panicking reinforces your false beliefs about the shadows. If you continue to believe that the shadows are sharks without verifying the clouds above or without listening to the people closest to you telling you to look up at the clouds, you'll continue to believe something that isn't true. You believe shadows in the water are sharks, and every time you see a shadow, you respond as if they're sharks. Your response reinforces your false belief. In time, you'll become afraid of all shadows in the water and feel fear every time you see the shadows. You believe something that isn't objectively true, but you feel and act as if it is true.

We can also believe things that others say about us that aren't true, which then causes us to behave in ways that affirm what's not true. Self-limiting mental habits are formed by false beliefs. In these moments, you can forget to pay attention to reality and what is true. Instead, you pay attention to your recurring thoughts that may be detached from reality, giving more weight to what others say about you rather than considering the objective truth.

The problem with your mental habits is you can misjudge the moments that prompt your habitual response, and you can assume that the outcome of your habits is always good. You no longer pay attention to what you do. You can habitually respond to beliefs and thoughts that aren't true, and you can wrongly believe that what you habitually do is good to do. You no longer focus on believing facts or the truth of the moment because you accept what is repeated as always true or good to do.

Everything begins with your beliefs. Your beliefs support your habits. When a person hears the sound of a gun or fireworks, for example, how they respond to it depends on what they know and believe about the firing of a gun. For runners, the sound of a gun is the signal to start running a race, while for people not accustomed to a starter gun, it's a signal that leads to running for safety. One signal, a gunshot in this case, can lead to people doing two separate things based on what they know and believe about the signal.

You can manage your habits for success by discovering the beliefs and thoughts that support your habits. We will dive into your repeated habits in the next chapter.

Notes

Notes

CHAPTER 2

HABITS

James's wife, Mary, is a nurse manager with an advanced practice degree. Mary wakes up every morning with little time to spare, inevitably causing her to rush. After making her morning coffee, she notices the kitchen is a mess but needs to leave for work, or she'll be late. On the road for only a few minutes, she realizes she has forgotten her lunch. It's too late to go back for it, so she'll have to eat out, which hinders her goal of saving money and time. Eating out also means she'll have less food variety, which hinders her diet goals. When she comes home, the kitchen is still a mess, and today, it's her turn to make dinner. She says to herself that tomorrow will be better and that she'll wake up earlier to exercise. At night, before bed, Mary begins scrolling through social media, and it's now later than she thought. She falls asleep, thinking she's sleeping at a good time. The next morning, the alarm on her phone turns on, and she presses snooze. She eventually wakes up at the same time she did yesterday, and she's still tired. It takes longer to get up than the previous day. She finally drags herself out of bed as the morning continues in the same hurried way it did yesterday. She tells herself again, as she rushes out the door with her coffee, that tomorrow will be different.

Habits Help or Hinder What You Want to Achieve

You may relate to this common problem: You want to achieve a goal, but your habits interfere with achieving that goal. What you do is not what you want, and what you want is not what you do. Like Mary, you want to be more productive, less distracted, eat healthier, exercise more, save more money, advance in your career, be more confident, make more friends, or achieve any other goal, but the things you repeatedly do (or don't do) seem to get in the way of achieving your goals.

You want to achieve your potential. But you encounter the common problem of giving up, not starting, changing your mind quickly, doing the things you shouldn't do, and not doing the things you should do. You get frustrated and begin to doubt your potential. You feel life is passing you by.

Habits are powerful actions that help or hinder you from achieving your potential, leading you closer to or further from achieving your goals. They are small acts that make a big difference. Your habits are stubborn, and if you're not aware of what you repeatedly do, it can hinder what you *want* to do. But habits are only a problem if you want something *different* from what you do. If you're happy with what you repeatedly do, then no changes are needed. Not all habits are bad, and much of your success in life is due to your good habits, helping you toward this stage in life. Yet you may still want to become better. If you're reading this book because you want to improve, know that in order to achieve anything different from what you're used to, you will need to improve your habits.

Habits Are What You Repeatedly Do

What are habits? Habits are like your washing machine. A washing machine has different settings programmed to run in a specific way, and each setting achieves a particular purpose by following a specific pattern. The clothes move in a cycle because the machine is programmed to spin them in a particular cycle. Every time you press a setting like normal, heavy-duty, or permanent press, the machine always does the same predictable thing. With every setting on your machine, there's a pattern that's regularly followed.

Similarly, when a trigger is pressed with your habits, you also do the same thing. You repeat the same pattern. The purpose of a washing machine is to clean your clothes so you're comfortable wearing something that makes you feel good. Habits have a purpose too, and it's to achieve what they repeat. Your habits are learned to achieve something. But not all the clothes you wash are the same in design, fabric, or purpose. Every piece of clothing is different and unique. There have been many times I've washed a white, expensive shirt only to receive a pink shirt! There have been many times I've washed my wife's exercise clothes, only to discover that they're much smaller in size than when I first placed them in the washer. I tend to wash all my clothes in the same way. I do this because the washing machine is so easy to use, and I'm lazy in not paying attention to what I wash. Our habits are also easy, and we are often lazy in not noticing what we repeatedly do.

You know your habits as the things you frequently tend to repeat. But there's a little more to them. Your habits are what you frequently and automatically tend to do in particular moments. There is always a relationship between two things in any habit: a situation you've experienced before and an act you repeat when that situation happens. The result is you do the same thing when a particular moment arises. What you repeat and when you do it are, therefore, familiar to you.

You tend to see habits in two different ways. First, habits are what you have. These are the things you tend to frequently and automatically do, such as negative self-talk. Second, habits are what you *want* to have. These are the things you desire to do automatically and consistently: exercising daily, sleeping more hours, reading (and finishing!) more books, saving money, meditating, journaling, sticking to a diet, being productive, and waking up at 5:00 a.m. When used in the second way, we want to do things as easily as we repeat our habits. We want to do them automatically.

The automatic repetition of your habits is what makes them consistent and powerful, but it's also their weakness. You want to "set it and forget it," but you often set a habit and *forget* what you're doing. When you are no longer paying attention to your repeated actions, this can lead to you doing something habitually that leads you further from achieving your potential. Returning to our washing machine illustration, if you wash all your clothes in the same way, you don't pay attention to the differences in the clothes you wash. You can ruin something delicate by habitually washing everything in the same way. Similarly, by not paying attention to what you habitually do, you can ruin or miss many opportunities to improve toward achieving your potential. Just as you can habitually believe that all the clothes can be washed in the same way, you can habitually believe that all of life's opportunities and situations are the same, while, in fact, they are not. Your clothes are unique, and so are your opportunities in life.

You Have Daily Habits

Habits are easily repeated and feel normal. You've done them for so long you don't think about them, and you're now accustomed to them. They are part of your daily life, and they're repeated *without* any thoughtful deliberation. Since habits are what you repeatedly do, they influence the direction of your day and life. You aren't aware of many of your habits unless you pay attention to when they occur or examine all the repeated things you do— or someone points them out to you. Here are some examples of under-the-radar daily habits:

- Checking your email, social media, or news as soon as you wake up
- Checking your social media in the presence of people
- Checking the news every hour or whenever you pick up your phone
- Checking the news, email, or social media before sleeping
- Constantly checking your phone for notifications
- Always having a warm cup of coffee or tea next to you

- Smoking, drinking, touching your hair, or doing something physical when stressed
- Looking down or slouching when meeting people
- Saying no to every opportunity that makes you uncomfortable
- Saying yes to everything
- Online shopping
- Comparing yourself to others
- Saying everything that enters your mind
- Always being late to things
- Debating people online
- Hoarding clothes, books, or boxes of miscellaneous things
- Binge-watching shows
- Always searching for random information online
- Lying
- Blaming others
- Judging others
- Complaining about everything
- Buying things you don't need
- Not eating or forgetting to eat
- Pushing people away or not allowing them to get close to you
- Always saying you're busy
- Interrupting people when they're speaking

You might identify with some of the habits above. Are there any additional daily habits you can think of that you frequently do? Look closely at all of your actions within a typical day; if done repeatedly and automatically in particular moments, they're done from habit.

You Have Work Habits

Your workplace is a great environment to learn your habits and the habits of others. Every week, you generally do the same job and see the same people.

The following are examples of work habits you may identify with, and some are identical to your daily habits:

- Checking your work inbox and work calendar as soon as you wake up
- Constantly checking your phone for notifications
- Checking your work inbox before sleeping
- Scrolling through social media during meetings, while replying to emails, or working on tasks
- Replying to emails on your phone while using the restroom
- Wanting to lead every meeting or video conference call and not giving others an opportunity to lead them
- Using the same vague phrases in meetings assuming everyone understands the meaning
- Interrupting others when they're speaking
- Taking credit for other people's work or not giving them explicit credit
- Under-sharing or not speaking during meetings because you're afraid of what people will think
- Oversharing and not thinking about what you say
- Constantly checking LinkedIn to see who's getting promoted

- Scrolling your inbox emails, not making decisions, and letting them accumulate
- Wanting to read and reply to every email to achieve "inbox zero"
- Typing quickly and correcting the many typos
- Keeping the same employee weekly calls when participation is low
- Having recurring meetings when there's nothing new to discuss
- Wanting to catch employees doing something wrong to discipline them
- Leading in the same way when the times require leading in a different way
- Using meetings to read from a presentation deck instead of using them to solve problems or explore opportunities
- Making excuses for bad results by blaming the times you're in or comparing yourself to someone who's doing worse to make your results look better

Work routines require you to do *something* consistently, and in doing something, your habits are revealed. In leadership, your habits are visibly expressed. Doing *something* reveals and expresses yourself. Doing *nothing* hides yourself. How you approach and do your job expresses and reveals a lot about you. For example, as a leader, you hold regular meetings. Meetings, which are often a product of habit, are one of the most consistent activities done in a business, so they tend to reflect habitual patterns. What habits do you repeat during meetings? What do you frequently and automatically do? Do you ask each team member for feedback on the discussion item, or do you reveal only what you think? Do you call on certain people frequently and ignore others? Do you do most of the talking during meetings? Do you interrupt people when they're speaking? Do you rely on the same agenda outline? Do you read a presentation deck instead of having honest and meaningful conversations? Work activities like meetings reveal many of your habits.

Leadership roles encourage and require you to interact with people, and this interaction reveals your social habits. Consider the following leadership habits in the workplace:

- How you talk to employees
- Your thoughts toward others with higher or lower rank
- How you disagree with people
- Whether you recognize or ignore people's achievements
- Who you give attention to and who you ignore
- How you listen to feedback
- Whether you care to listen to someone's feedback
- Whether you show empathy when listening to others
- Whether you care to ask employees their name and learn about them
- Whether you remember the names of the people you lead
- Whether you isolate yourself in your leadership cliques (and exclude others)
- Who you always sit with and don't sit with
- Whether you multitask and remain distracted when people talk to you

People are promoted for being successful in a role, and their success reflects many of their successful habits. In a new role, people continue the same habits. It's very rare to reexamine your habits when entering into a new role. The primary focus becomes the new responsibilities that need to be achieved rather than any self-improvement prior to entering a new role. If you do examine and reflect upon your habits, it tends to happen during vacation periods or before entering a new year. Reevaluating your habits also happens during life events such the death of someone close to you, the birth of children, spiritual awakenings, advancing in age, illness, and children leaving home. When advancing into a new role or new project, you continue to do what you're comfortable with, and if what you do is good, you continue having success. But if you continue to do what doesn't work, then the outcome remains the same.

Stepping away from your work environment into a different environment, like a vacation, retreat, or "staycation," can help you become more aware of your habits, values, and purpose in life. You can reexamine how you use your time, evaluate what's most important to you, and achieve a different perspective on your repeated work activities. In this away-from-work environment, you can intentionally place the focus on yourself to review your values, goals, priorities, and direction. Your quiet moments can be your loudest and most memorable ones. Vacations give you the mental space to reorganize your values, goals, and activities, and they permit you to "reenter" work with a refreshed and more focused perspective. Vacations are underutilized in helping you become better. Working for a new company or team can also reveal the striking differences between what you did before and what you can do differently.

Your Habits Are Learned

You've developed habits to achieve something. To keep your teeth healthy (goal), you brush your teeth daily (habit). Habits are often accompanied by a feeling of satisfaction or pleasure and tend to feel good. For many people, drinking soda throughout the day is enjoyable. The outcome of drinking soda is pleasure and satisfaction. The outcome of belonging to a group is safety and a feeling of unity. The outcome of exercise is various health benefits. Most of the outcomes you desire have a reward.

There's something you want by repeating a habit—but not always. Sometimes you do something habitually that you don't want to do. For example, you can believe you're an intelligent person and full of potential, and yet when you walk into a room of leaders, you can suddenly lose confidence. You can believe you're highly intelligent yet believe you're not important in the presence of certain people. You doubt yourself, and the outcome is you lose your confidence in those situations. Why does this happen? You have a mental habit in response to a familiar situation. Why do you do what you don't want to do? Because of what you believe. You believe you're not as important as the people you doubt yourself with. By doubting yourself, you achieve the outcome of what you believe: that you're not important. By avoiding conversations with people, not sharing about yourself, and declining to share your thoughts with the group, your actions reaffirm and confirm your belief. Habits can form a vicious cycle of confirming things that aren't true.

Habits can also have more than one outcome. The outcome of drinking soda is both pleasure *and* the erosion of tooth enamel. You can achieve what you want and also achieve what you don't want. You can wake up at 5:00 a.m. because you believe *people who wake up at 5:00 a.m. are more productive* and then not realize that your lack of sleep is causing you mental and physical fatigue. Although you are productive first thing in the morning, your productivity is limited to a few morning hours, whereas the rest of your day is lost by being tired. You lose a full day's worth of productivity in exchange for a few hours. You may continue waking up at 5:00 a.m. because it validates your idea that waking up early means you're productive, while not realizing being tired the rest of the day is increasing your mistakes at work and lack of social engagement. You can fulfill one goal (waking up early) while also unknowingly hindering the fulfillment of another goal (being productive and attentive all day). Fulfilling one goal can hinder achieving your most important goals, and one habit can lead to the formation of other undesired habits. That's why it is so important to pay attention to what you do habitually.

Your habits are learned patterns of behavior. When a familiar moment happens, such as when an idea, desire, or impulse arises, there's something you frequently and automatically do. When you get angry, do you lash out or withdraw? When you're stressed, do you reach for food or alcohol? You may not always react to the motivating impulse, but when you do, you frequently do the same thing. Your habits are not a surprise because you've experienced the situation that prompts your response. The familiar moment can arise daily, monthly, or yearly, but when it does arise, you continue to do the same thing. It is not how frequently the situation presents itself but the fact that you respond in the same way whenever the situation arises.

There are certain triggers, signals, or cues you respond to that motivate your habits. Here are some examples:

- *Desires.* A desire is a powerful feeling that craves something. When you have a frequent desire, you can fulfill it with a habitual action. When a frequent desire arises, what do you repeatedly do?

- *Emotions.* When you feel various emotions, you can tend to behave in a habitual way. Is there something you repeatedly do when you feel happy, overwhelmed, angry, anxious, or stressed?

- *Boredom.* When you feel bored, you're disinterested. What do you automatically do when bored? Do you automatically pick up your phone and turn to social media? Do you scroll through the news, shop, or do anything else to alleviate your boredom?

- *Events.* There are certain situations that elicit the same response within you. If you exercise, do you feel bad about yourself when you see someone who's more fit than you? What moments and situations do you respond to in the same way?

- *Tasks and activities.* Do you do something in the same way because it's the best way or the way you've always done it?

- *People and places.* There are certain people or places you respond to in the same, habitual way. Do you tend to ignore employees with less rank by showing no interest in their lives? Do you show favoritism toward people you like by giving them preferential treatment? Do you promote more people to leadership positions who are from your same region, job group, or network?

Your habits are real in the sense that they are actions. But although your habits are real, they do not mean they're always true to reality or the best you can do. By understanding your habits are learned, you can begin taking greater control over them and the outcomes they produce.

You Can Make New Decisions

The reason you've learned your habits is to achieve a predictable outcome. What you believe about the repeated situation is what begins your habitual response. When you do your weekly grocery shopping, you likely visit the same places, spend a consistent amount of time (and money) at each location, and take the same routes. Your weekly patterns rarely change. Your habits are reliable. It's also easy to repeat your pattern. You don't have to think about it. You may notice your physical habits and not realize the thoughts behind your habits. Your habits seem to arise spontaneously and out of nowhere but are ingrained as the result of repetition. You're accustomed to repeating them. They feel normal. Since habits are what you frequently do, they help or hinder achieving your goals.

If your habits are what you desire and lead to a favorable outcome, then good. Keep repeating them. If your habits are not what you desire, then you can begin making changes. You can re-evaluate your habits. How do you make changes? The first step is acknowledging you have habits, both good and bad. Take an honest look at your habits, acknowledge you've learned to do something, and understand you can also change what you've learned to do. If you can't acknowledge you have bad habits, for example, nothing can change because you deny anything needs improvement. By not acknowledging your good habits, on the other hand, you can't appreciate all the small things you do consistently well and how they have led you to accomplish many wonderful things. You're a leader because of your good habits. You're reading this book *because* you have the habit of wanting to become better. Your life is filled with many good habits. It's important to acknowledge them and feel good about them.

When you acknowledge your habits, you recognize they're simply repeated actions in familiar moments. You recognize their power, but at the same time, you can limit their power by understanding that a repeated action can change. You can have more control over your habits instead of feeling that you're controlled by them. Your habits are learned, and they can be unlearned and changed.

Acknowledging your habits is acknowledging your power to change and improve them. Knowing how they work is knowing the limits to their power. You recognize them not as strangers to fear but as old friends to welcome. You know when they tend to arise and what you tend to do as a result of their triggers. You're not surprised by them or afraid of them. You look forward to improving them.

Habits are what you repeatedly do, but they are not who you are. Your habits are the product of your decisions, and you can begin making new decisions every day.

Notes

Notes

CHAPTER 3

THE INFLUENCE OF YOUR ENVIRONMENT

*The more time you spend with others,
the more you learn from them.*

J ames and Mary have been married for ten years and have two kids. They have a happy marriage, love their kids, and enjoy successful business careers. At home, when Mary is talking, she tends to talk loudly, while James is the opposite. He's fairly quiet, but when something bothers him, he gets upset that no one knows why he's upset. The family knows something bothers him when he begins to scrub the dinner dishes harder or doesn't say anything at dinner. When the kids misbehave, his first thought is what kind of consequences the kids need. For Mary, her first thought is to talk to the kids *without* delivering consequences. Mary is quick to judge other people and frequently says what she thinks. James doesn't judge others but never says anything he thinks.

James's father is quiet, not social, and would punish James for minor misdeeds. James has never had a close relationship with his father. James's mother is naturally compassionate, soft-spoken, and quiet around the house. Mary's mother is social, says what she thinks, and tends to look down on other people. Growing up, Mary's mother would mock her and say unflattering things about her appearance. Mary and her mother are close and love to talk about politics. Mary's father is an early riser, always punctual, and believes if you're not working on a house project, you're lazy.

As a married couple, James and Mary have become aware of what they habitually do, and although they get annoyed at each other's quirks, they make each other better people. They each remind the other when they begin to display habits that are not healthy for the relationship.

Your Environment Is a Source of Ideas

Your environment is the surroundings in which you live, work, and socialize, and it's the culture of influence you interact with. Your environment influences the way you experience and perceive the world. The way you feel at a quiet park on a sunny day, for example, is different from the way you feel sitting in an office on a sunny day. If you had a meeting and could choose to have it at a quiet park or in an office, what would you choose? Despite doing the same activity with the same content and conversations, a meeting would feel more enjoyable at the park because you would feel more comfortable and relaxed. On the other hand, looking at the squirrels could distract you, and you'd be better off inside a meeting room. Your surroundings influence your thoughts, beliefs, feelings, and behaviors. Your environment influences how you feel, as well as what you think and do.

Your group environment consists of people and exerts a strong influence over the formation of many of your beliefs and habits. You can trace many of your habits to the significant people in your upbringing and to the group environments to which you belong. It's often a primary source of ideas and information about yourself, others, and the world. This is significant, as the ideas you accept as true become your beliefs, and what you believe influences your direction in life, your everyday decisions, and your habits. When you accept an idea from others, and that idea is about *anything*—acceptable behavior, leadership responsibilities, parental responsibilities, gender roles, racial stereotypes, the qualifications for a new candidate—you begin forming habits when you respond to that idea in a repetitive way. You then do the same thing when the familiar moment happens.

If you believe that leaders should begin every meeting with opening comments, for example, then you begin *every* meeting with opening comments even if you're not leading the meeting or providing new content. You rearrange your busy calendar just to provide opening comments. Introducing a topic so *someone else* can talk about the topic is an accepted idea that's frequently repeated. But the result is valuable time is unnecessarily used for the key leaders and the employees within the meeting.

The ideas you accept from others about what to do or believe form many of your habits, just as the information you receive and accept from others helps form your beliefs. Some of what you habitually do is taught to you by others or learned by observing them. You were taught to brush your teeth twice daily as a child, and now it's a habit. You do it automatically upon rising and going to sleep. You were taught to look both ways when crossing the street, and now you do it automatically. What you're taught to do can come from knowledgeable people. You trust them because of their knowledge, and their knowledge helps you in some way. At other times, what you're taught comes from people who are not experts. They share their opinions, but their opinions can be biased and incorrect, which can lead to you accepting biased or incorrect ideas about yourself, others, and the world. You can, in turn, develop habits in response to ideas that aren't true to reality.

What you learn from others is important to consider because it impacts the direction of your life. Your group environment can become your entire reality. You can become so immersed in your career, political group, religious group, professional group, or ethnic group that you see the world only from within the ideas, beliefs, and culture of the group. You, therefore, don't see the world *as it is* and instead see it as people within the group *say* it is. Your group environment can be the only people you interact with, and because of that exclusivity, they can have a tremendous influence on your ideas about yourself, others, and the world. For many people, their group environment *is* their reality. Living within an enclosed circle of the same ideas and experiences is popularly described as "living in a bubble." How you experience the world, your attitude and beliefs toward others and yourself, the customs you repeat, the expectations you develop, and the habits you form are all influenced by your environment and, in particular, your group environment.

Your Upbringing Influences Your Beliefs and Habits

People are a big part of your environment, and they play a significant role in creating your habits. Your first experience with a group environment was during your formative years, so many of your strongest habits were likely acquired during that time. For a portion of your life, your family is the most meaningful environment you experience, and they are your most consistent source of ideas and information about yourself and others. Your family upbringing affects your beliefs and habits by what you learn and accept from them. You see the same people daily over the course of years, and you're constantly learning and observing as you develop into adulthood. Every family environment has a culture of beliefs, expectations, and customs, and you acquire beliefs and habits as a response to events within your family upbringing.

The beliefs you acquired during your upbringing have led to many of your current habits or your propensity to form certain habits. In your upbringing, you're seeing the same behavior loop from others and constantly hearing the same ideas. If you have a negative or optimistic attitude, are judgmental, find it difficult to establish close relationships, make excuses, feel inferior or superior to others, smoke or drink, raise your voice, say everything that comes to mind, or have a quick temper, you likely picked these up from your family upbringing. During my childhood, for example, I grew up in a low-income area in Los Angeles. There were car thefts, vehicle crashes, and graffiti in the community.

My mother would never let me stay out past 10:00 p.m. because she believed there was too much danger in the neighborhood. To verify her belief, I watched the nightly news. The majority of the nightly news content focused on criminal activity, police pursuits, kidnappings, or some sad event. (It wasn't until I was older that I realized the nightly news focuses on selective content to keep people engaged.) The nightly news supported what I had learned from my mother. I believed there was danger in the neighborhood every time I stayed out till dark, and I would run home and avoid certain blocks at night. If I saw a person walking toward me, I would cross the street to avoid them. This meant I took longer routes to get home. To this day, I carry many of my childhood fears, and I have the same fears for my children. Although I live in a safe neighborhood, I still double-check that all the doors and windows are locked every night. *Every night.* Even so, I continually remind myself not to pass on the habitual thoughts of danger I learned to my kids.

There are all sorts of beliefs you're taught by others in your upbringing, beliefs about yourself, others, and the world, that influence both your habits and behavior toward yourself and others. In your upbringing, you don't have the personal experiences to verify the truth of what you're told, so you naturally believe it and behave accordingly.

One of the strongest habitual patterns from your upbringing that continues throughout your life is the process of conditioning—when someone wants you to respond or think in a certain way based on the ideas and information they give you. With conditioning, you develop a strong association between an idea and a desired reaction. Conditioning is more intentional than learning behavior by observing and interacting with others. Sometimes what you're conditioned to believe and do is good— such as when you're taught to get underneath a desk during an earthquake or pull to the side of the road when you hear the siren of a first responder. But sometimes, you're conditioned to believe ideas that are not good, such as when you're taught to believe negative things about yourself or others. Someone may *want* you to feel bad about yourself or hostile toward others.

Sometimes conditioning is done for entertainment. For example, I visited a well-known amusement park in California, and while waiting in the back of the line for one of the rides, the music was dark, scary, and ominous. The lights within the building were low with a gloomy look. But as I got closer to the front of the line, the music became heroic, the decorations on the wall inspired courage, and a character on the screen gave encouraging words to the people waiting in line. The message the ride wanted you to believe was that you're a hero. The theme ride environment did what it was supposed to do: create fear and courage by causing the people in line to respond to carefully selected music, words, lighting, and decorations. The theme park ride wanted me to *respond* in a certain way based on what they *presented* to me, and I responded exactly how they wanted me to respond.

Conditioning happens in all areas of life. If you attend religious services, the customs that attendees follow and repeat are learned through conditioning. In the same way, negative or cynical thinking ("everything is bad"), self-criticism ("I'm undeserving"), and boastful pride ("I'm better than everyone") are often habitual attitudes learned by the ideas and information offered within your upbringing. Your attitude and patterns of thinking are conditioned by the ideas and information presented to you.

The ideas and beliefs you accept and learn from others lead to many of your habits. Habits have outcomes since they're repeated actions, and what you were taught to do in your upbringing has outcomes. Two things happen when repeating your conditioned habits. First, your habitual pattern reinforces the idea you're taught and accepted. Whenever the situation arises that prompts your habitual response, that idea of what to do is reinforced and further strengthened within you. What you do reinforces what to do next time. Again, going back to the religious services example, every time the customs are repeated, the link between what to do becomes stronger. You begin to do it without thinking about it. Second, your habitual pattern leads to a known outcome. You want to feel a certain way, or someone else wants you to feel a certain way by how you habitually respond. When you participate in religious customs, there's a positive emotion that arises. You know how you're going to feel every time you participate. The feelings also affirm your beliefs about what you repeat. When standing in line at the theme ride in an amusement park, you feel anticipation when the ride music is played. You get more excited as you move closer to the front of the line. No amusement park wants you to *avoid* moving to the front of the line. If you're told in your upbringing (or group environment) that you have no talents, and you accept that idea, whenever a promotion opportunity arises at work, you'll tend to automatically think you're not qualified for the position or that someone else is better for it than you. You're *inclined* to think that way because of what you've accepted as true, although you may still apply for the promotion because you *want* something different.

The problem with not evaluating the ideas you accept from others is they can be false, morally wrong, or have a repeated outcome you don't want. You can accept false ideas about yourself that then cause you to limit your potential. You can accept ideas that don't work but continue because they're repeated by influential people. The fact that everyone else is doing it, or that someone with authority said it, or that it's been done in a certain way for a long time does not mean it's good to do, the best thing to do, or correct. Repetition doesn't make a bad idea a good idea. Repetition doesn't make a false idea a true idea. But the repetition of a good and truthful idea can lead to long-lasting success and the achievement of your potential.

Groups Influence Your Beliefs and Habits

A second significant part of your environment is your social group. These are the people you spend time with or closely follow because you have something in common.

Similar to your upbringing, your social groups influence your beliefs and habits by what you learn and accept from them. In a social group environment, habits are visible through the customs and expectations of the group. There are examples you learn from and expectations you accept. Your group environment is a source of ideas and information and, therefore, a source of your ideas, beliefs, and habits. If you've ever heard the phrase,

"That's how we've always done it," then you've experienced habitual expectations in a group setting.

The following are some examples of social groups:

- Professional associations
- Religious communities
- Political groups
- The military
- Law enforcement
- Groups formed around a common interest, such as sports, hobbies, outdoor activities, etc.
- Your circle of friends
- Your coworkers
- Family members
- Business resource groups within a company

There are also media personalities, influential people ("influencers"), and authors you listen to, read, and follow closely. There's always someone you're interacting with, learning from, and identifying with. The draw of social groups is the sense of unity and commonality you find with others, as you share common characteristics, interests, beliefs, and experiences. There is often a group language, appearance, and rules ("codes") unique to the group. You can belong to many social groups at the same time.

Your workplace environment is a social group. In belonging to a company, for example, you belong to a group of people with a common mission to provide products and services to society. There are expectations, values, and a common identity that come with belonging to the company. As a principle of social inter-action, you're prone to take on the habits and attitudes of the people you spend the most time with or deeply associate with. This principle is even stronger when interacting with a leader or a person of authority. You can acquire their ideas, beliefs, and habits and repeat them without intending to. If you're part of the leadership of the business, for example, and every executive reads a book a month, you'll likely take on that behavior as well.

Groups Help Form Your Identity

You can find meaning, purpose, and self-worth when belonging to a group. You tend to take on the identity of the groups you associate with, or you use the groups you identify with to express your identity. For example, if you enjoy sports, you may associate with your favorite sports team *as if* you are part of the team. Do you ever yell at the screen if your team makes a mistake, misses a shot, or loses? Do you scream in excitement if your team does something good? You get excited when they win and upset when they lose, even though you're not playing, and the players don't know who you are. If you've ever had a conversation with some-one about sports and you say, "I can't believe we lost yesterday!" or "We are going to win this year!" or "The team sucks this year!" or "I would have made that shot!!" then you've identified yourself with a group. You associate yourself with being part of the team. Anytime you catch yourself using the word "we" to discuss the group you belong to or "they" to discuss the group you distin-guish yourself from, then you identify yourself with a group.

Social groups are important because they can define your identity by the ideas, beliefs, and customs you accept from them. The group becomes your identity. You can believe your identity is more important by taking on the larger identity of the group.

Groups Set Expectations

In a group environment, leaders set the standard of what's acceptable and not acceptable to repeat, and it's usually a small, insular group that sets the expectations and standards for others to follow. A person with a very strong personality can define the identity of the group. You can see this happening within political circles, religious circles, and business circles, where one strong personality and their prevailing ideas become widely accepted within the group, and their ideas become a standard for others to follow. For example, in a group setting, if leaders display behavior that's generally not acceptable, like cursing, you find it more acceptable to display that behavior, especially if others begin to display it as well. But if you're the leader with social authority and a peer curses in a meeting, the group looks to you for approval or disapproval of the displayed behavior. If you disapprove, no one else will curse in the meeting. Leaders set the standard for acceptable behavior and expectations.

Sometimes you acquire the habits of others to be accepted by them. You believe that if you're like them, they will like you. By repeating what others do, you repeat it to be affirmed. Other times, you repeat the behavior of others because you hope to have the same outcome or results. Repeating what's accepted leads to repeating what's expected.

Common phrases you may often hear repeated in a meeting:

- We need air cover
- What's the major and the minor?
- Is it scalable?
- It's a new muscle to flex
- We need a hands-on approach
- Punt it
- Definable and repeatable
- Level up
- Lean in
- Line of sight
- Drill down
- What's your why?
- Get tactical

When you hear these phrases repeatedly from someone you admire, you can begin to subconsciously repeat the same phrases during the meeting or carry them to other meetings. By repeating the leadership language, you find acceptance and unity with the group even if the outcome of the habit is unclear communication.

We are prone to subconsciously acquire the habits of others within a social group to be accepted by them, find approval, achieve unity, and achieve a similar outcome to the habits we observe and repeat.

Groups Establish a Culture

When you belong to a social group, you belong to a group culture—a collection of customs, shared beliefs, ideas, and expectations. Group culture is a shared experience that helps define the group identity, and it has its own unique communication style. Anytime there's a group, there's a culture of shared ideas, expectations, and behaviors. Your family and home have a culture. Your workplace has a culture. Your favorite sports team, your religious affiliation, the political group you identify with, the military, and law enforcement all have a culture. If you lead a business, or lead a team, you have the power to establish the culture.

Culture is created. Culture is kept alive by repeating it or by doing nothing to change it. When people say their work is a "toxic culture," what they mean is it's an environment with harmful ideas, beliefs, language, and behavior. It's an environment that *repeats* harmful beliefs, and behavior. If you were to change jobs and start at a different company, for example, one of your former peers is likely to ask you, "How do you like the culture of your new job? What's the culture like?" You've likely also asked the same question of your former colleagues who have gone on to work for different companies. When asking someone, "What's it like to work there?" or how they like their new job, you're asking them what the culture and group environment are like. Your surroundings, whether it's one influential person or a group of like-minded people, influence many of your beliefs and habits because of the ideas and expectations you accept.

Thinking Differently from Your Environment

Although you learn ideas from your environment, it does not mean you always share the same ideas. There are times when you disagree with the prevailing ideas, or you want to know *why* certain things are done if you're expected to follow in the repetition. There are also moments when you have your own ideas that you want to share and contribute. Disagreeing, wanting an explanation, and sharing your thoughts are signs that you're paying attention to your environment. You're thinking and being aware of your surroundings, deciding for yourself if what's repeatedly done is worthwhile to accept based on what you know to be true.

Sometimes you gain perspective by stepping *out* of your environment. You can develop new ideas, beliefs, and habits that are contrary to your group environment by interacting with a new environment. When you interact with different people—reading a biography, attending meetings where people share ideas, or interacting with people that aren't within your group environment—you acquire new experiences. You learn fresh perspectives and gain additional knowledge. It's the nature of a social group to repeat the same experiences, ideas, beliefs, and habits. This is what makes social groups so reliable, and it's also what can make them repeat ideas and activities that don't reflect reality, don't work, have lost their meaning, or exclude new ideas and activities that can improve the group.

You become *more* aware of what you do by experiencing a new environment because you observe and learn what others do. There is a contrast and comparison that occurs similar to when you subconsciously compare yourself with others. When people attend yearly meetings for the professional associations they belong to, for example, it's typical to come back with new ideas to implement or with resolutions to change something. New and different group environments are significant because they provide you with contrast and comparison to your group environment. You've likely changed some of your views as you've grown older because you've experienced more of life and the perspectives of other people. You think differently now than ten years ago. You no longer hold onto certain beliefs and habits you strongly embraced ten years ago, and in the next ten years, some of your beliefs and habits may continue to change based on what you experience. You hold on to some, discard others, and accept new beliefs and habits as you grow in life. New environments bring new ideas and experiences that challenge or affirm your ideas, beliefs, and habits.

Disagreement happens when your beliefs interact with your environment. There are various ways this can happen. One way is you can simply disagree with the prevailing ideas and beliefs, thinking differently than what's being presented to you. When presented with conflicting ideas, you must decide if you'll accept or decline what's presented to you. Some of the greatest moments you can hope for are when your ideas are challenged because they can open the door to exceptional growth. Disagreement should not be feared.

A second way is you simply want things that are *different* from what your environment and culture present to you. You're not satisfied, and you're looking for something more. This can happen when you're frustrated with the lack of good solutions to the common problems of your environment. You're tired of the same thing. You want something better, and you have your own ideas. You're willing to do something about it.

If you disagree with how leaders run a meeting, for example, this disagreement can strengthen your own ideas of how meetings should run effectively. People can also disagree with how you run your meetings, especially if you repeat things that are not relevant to the problems and opportunities of the present moment. Every leader has habits they're blind to but are obvious to others.

Disagreeing with your environment can help change your mind, or it can *strengthen* your mind. You can double down on your ideas and beliefs when you believe other people are wrong, or you can become more stubborn when you're afraid to be wrong. Disagreeing with others does not mean you're always right. If you don't get the promotion you wanted, for example, you can remain insistent that you're the better candidate and build resentment toward the person who received the promotion and the person who gave the promotion. A failure to admit disappointment is a failure to accept reality, and it's important to be honest with the reality of a situation.

Sometimes, disagreement leads you to believe *less* strongly than before, and this can result in *openness* to new ideas and perspectives. In our example of not getting the promotion, you could accept reality, acknowledge someone else was chosen, choose to work and collaborate with them, continue to improve, and continue to remain open to new opportunities—instead of getting angry. You then become an optimistic person because of the growth you can control. The person who was promoted ahead of you can become your bridge to new opportunities. One thing you can be certain of is that life changes. Disappointment and mental conflicts in what you believe can create a good, positive change in the direction of your life—as well as the best moments of your life.

Thinking differently from your environment can be helpful, as it can help change your direction and help you become a better leader. Disagreement is a sign that you're thinking about what you observe. It helps change or strengthen your ideas, beliefs, and habits. If your team disagrees with an idea, policy, practice, or custom, you should welcome the observation as it can point you closer to the truth of the matter.

Group Expectations Can Be Good

Expectations lead you to do something, and one of the benefits of a good environment is the expectation of what *should be*. Good expectations help you reach further toward achieving your goals, and as you strive forward, new expectations arise that seemed unattainable before. Expectations are necessary to achieve growth. You may not appreciate the stress or demands of your work environment, but some stress is necessary for growth. For people who have a habit of *procrastination*, for example, this habit can be visible in one area of life and not the other. When at work, you can be productive, focused, motivated, and have friends. You can wake up with no problem. But at home, you can struggle to wake up on your days off. You can feel unproductive, doom scroll on your mobile phone for useless information, put projects and tasks off for another day, and not have any control over your routines or habits. But when you're back to work, you're again pushing yourself to achieve your goals. The differences between the two environments are the expectations, accountability, and obligations that you have at work and not at home. Expectations make a difference.

The expectations of your group environment are good if they lead to something worthwhile. Group expectations become difficult to accept, however, when they're meant to support ideas, beliefs, habits, and activities that aren't true, harmful, don't work, or exclude a person's individuality. Group expectations should never take a person's individuality away because being different is what makes someone unique and significant. It is a person's uniqueness that produces a different perspective and new ideas. If someone in the group has an idea to share, especially if it's a contrary opinion, pay attention to the content and merits of the idea, and not solely on their social status.

Think About What You Learn and Accept from Others

Not everything you believe comes from direct knowledge or experience. You learn ideas, expectations, and customs from your group environment. My wife, for instance, culturally believes specific colors bring good luck and bad luck. She takes precautions with the colors she wears, whereas I don't. But despite wearing good-luck colors, she still has bad days at work, yet she continues to believe in the charm of colors. The ideas you accept from others give direction to your everyday life.

You take many of the ideas and beliefs in your environment and culture for granted and believe they're right. It doesn't mean they're wrong; it means many are not personally verified. You accept they're right because the leaders and people share them, and you've used them to navigate life. Since many of your beliefs are learned from the people and groups you identify with and belong to, you can often accept them without deep consideration and simply trust what you accept. You take *action* based on what you or the group believe is important and true. You express habits when you automatically do what's repeated or expected. You develop habits by learning and accepting from others what to repeatedly think and do.

You trust your group environment. But if you assume that the ideas, beliefs, and habits of your environment are always correct, you will also accept their bad ideas, beliefs, and habits. You will repeat what others do without thinking about if what you repeat is good or worthwhile. You can then easily repeat people's mistakes, biases, and bad decisions.

Leaders are people that make mistakes, and because of their position, they can become detached from the reality that their people experience. Leaders receive ideas and information from others, and what they receive can be biased, wrong, or outdated. Leaders make bad decisions when they receive bad information. A doctor, for example, can misdiagnose a patient's disease if they receive the wrong data from blood tests or scans. A military field leader can pursue the wrong target if they receive inaccurate intelligence. A manager can focus on the wrong reasons for bad results based on the feedback they receive. Yet even if you receive accurate information, your biases can lead you to agree with the selective information that supports the outcome you want. It's easy to see only what you want to see. A position of power gives

54

leaders priority in making decisions, but it does not mean their ideas and decisions are always correct or true.

Pay attention to the ideas you accept from others and think about if they're true or worthy to accept. It's always easier to accept ideas about yourself, others, and the world from the people closest to you or within your environment without thinking about what you accept. But if your goal is to achieve your potential, make the best decisions, do the right activities, and always know the truth, you must pay attention to what you accept from others.

Notes

Notes

CHAPTER 4

SELF-AWARENESS

If you're aware of what you repeatedly do,
you can determine what you want to do.

J ames is not the handiest person in the house. When things break or need replacement, he calls his father-in-law, brothers, friends, or a repairman—always in that order according to who's available. He repairs and replaces things only when they cease to work and not when they start showing signs of deterioration. As a result of waiting, he always spends more on replacing things than fixing them. He never pays for warranties, and when things break, he always tells himself, "I should have got a warranty." James has a long commute to work. When he hears a noise in the vehicle, he ignores it until the noise gets louder. When at the repair shop, he always asks, "How long can I wait before I really need to repair the problem?" He always pays more by waiting. On a recent car servicing appointment, he was told his four tires needed replacement. He replied by saying

DANNY ZELAYA

he felt he had *just* bought new tires a year ago. He was asked if he noticed the car drifting one way while driving, and he said he did notice it drifting toward the driver's side. He didn't think that was a big deal. At the end of the appointment, James paid for four new tires and a vehicle alignment. James again paid more by waiting to fix things.

***

When driving a vehicle over time, your wheels can become misaligned. Your vehicle begins to drift one way when you're meaning to drive straight. You may think this is normal because you drive your vehicle so much, and you can't remember when the vehicle didn't drift one way. Drifting one way can seem harmless, but a misaligned vehicle causes the tires to wear out quickly, the gas mileage to drop, the parts attached to your wheel to become damaged, and, most importantly, misalignment hinders your goal of driving safely. Aligning your vehicle ensures you're driving straight and in the direction you want. An aligned vehicle helps achieve full performance.

Similarly, you have habits that pull you one way. You drift in the direction of your habits. What frequently happens feels normal, and you drift toward what you repeat. Are your habits aligned in the direction you want, or do they pull you in a direction you don't want?

Keeping your vehicle functioning to its full performance requires basic maintenance. Keeping yourself functioning to your full potential also requires basic maintenance. To change your habits, you first need to be *aware* of them. Self-awareness is needed for self-improvement. Without self-awareness, you don't know what you habitually do, and without personal responsibility, you can't achieve what you want to do.

> Take responsibility for your habits by paying
> attention to what you habitually do and
> what you want to do. Make a decision.

Start by Asking Questions & Paying Attention

Self-awareness is a mental pause. It's having conscious knowledge of yourself. You become aware of anything you want to notice in the present moment—your thoughts, feelings, breathing, and, yes, your habits. When self-aware of your habits, you slow down to pay attention to what you repeatedly do in familiar moments. You notice when you're inclined to repeatedly do something. You learn to observe when your habits arise. You notice yourself to know yourself.

When you visit a coffee shop for the first time, you patiently look at the menu. You want to see what looks good and what can satisfy your appetite. If you can't make a decision by the time you order, you sometimes ask the host for what they recommend or what's popular on the menu. Let's say you order something good that you enjoy. The next time you visit, you may spend a little time reviewing the menu again, but you'll likely order the same thing as before. Over time, the more you visit, you know what you want without thinking about it. You don't notice the new options on the menu. You no longer pay attention to the menu at all. You order what you frequently select, and if the people at the coffee shop know you, you'll likely say, "I'll get the usual," and they'll repeat your order from memory.

Habits make life easy because you don't have to spend mental energy deliberating every decision. Habits give you one less thing to think about. But it is precisely because habits are easy that we forget about what we repeatedly do. You order the same coffee drink without looking at the menu. You assume the menu doesn't change. You assume the situation that prompts your habitual response is the same as before. That's why you repeat the same action when a familiar situation arises. But the life outside of your mind *does* change, and if you assume everything is the same, you can misjudge or miss many opportunities by not paying attention. Habits can reflect your past, so you need to discover if what you repeatedly do is good for you to continue doing—or even what you *want* to do. Are you aware of what you repeatedly do? Are you happy with the outcome of your habits? Are your habits true to reality?

How do you become aware of your habits? There are two things you can do. First, *ask yourself questions*, and second, *pay attention* to yourself during certain moments. First, ask yourself, "What do I habitually do?" or "What do I automatically respond to in the same way?" These two questions bring attention to your repeated actions. In recognizing your repeated actions, you can identify the repeating thoughts that motivate your habitual patterns. By asking yourself the two questions, you may be introspective enough that you come up with the most important habits you want to improve. But if your mind is still blank, there's another way to ask yourself the same questions. Identify what you want to improve *and then* pay attention to any habits that hinder you.

Try naming the different areas of your life you want to improve by identifying habits. For example: "What do I habitually do at work, in meetings, with my kids, while exercising, in my relationships, in my free time, when asked to take a risk, or when someone upsets me?" Write down the most important areas you want to improve and think about the habits you can make better.

Here are some examples of goals you may have:

- Improve my communication in meetings
- Improve my time management
- Improve my peer relationships or relationship with someone
- Improve toward a promotion
- Exercise more often
- Improve my work productivity
- Sleep more hours

Let's focus on improving *peer relationships*. Let's say you want to be more patient and kind with someone in the workplace. That's your goal. Begin by asking yourself, "What are the things I habitually do toward this person?" or "What do I automatically respond to in the same way?" You interact with many people during the day; you talk with them about life, work with them, and laugh together, but when you interact with the person

63

you want to have a better relationship with, you notice that *how* you respond to them is *different* from the way you respond to everyone else. You ignore them, or you're abrupt and get quickly irritated with them even if they ask you the same question everyone else asks you. You also don't ask them the same questions about work or life that you ask everyone else. This is what hinders achieving your goal of improving the relationship. You've identified your *bad* habit within the goal you want to achieve.

If you remember from Chapter 1, beliefs support your habits. Ask yourself *why* you habitually respond to this person in the same way. What do you *believe* about them that causes you to respond in the same habitual way? Do you believe they're not as important as you? Are you perhaps jealous of the attention they receive or envious of their success? You approach them with the same attitude, which is a habit. You don't notice that most of your interactions with the person are good. You don't allow the good moments to change your outlook because you assume that every experience with the person *will* be bad. Your mental habit creates a bad perception that you believe, even if it's not true to reality.

Let's now focus on a second example. Let's say you want to improve your *time management*. That's your goal. Begin by asking yourself, "What do I repeatedly do that hinders my time management?" "What do I automatically respond to in the same way that eats up my time?" The answers here can range from too much time on social media, the internet, reading every email, or constantly being distracted by your coworkers. You identify that you have the habit of saying "yes" to everything. You agree to join every meeting or call you're invited on. You agree to every project or task that's presented to you. You agree to every request of your time. You have the habit of saying "yes" because you're uncomfortable saying "no." You discover that you can't manage your time wisely because you're being managed by everything you say "yes" to.

You can improve the achievement of your goals by identifying the habits that hinder your progress. If you don't address your bad habits, they remain with you and can hinder you from developing new ones. Bad habits don't disappear by ignoring them. A golfer that has the habit of overswinging must correct the habit by shortening their swing rather than adding the new habit of showing up to the range more often. Developing the new habit of taking more swings will not correct the habit of overswinging and will, in fact, make the bad habit worse. People excessively focus on what *new* habits to develop to be successful and don't work on changing their existing habits. It can be uncomfortable and painful acknowledging your bad habits. But without acknowledging and changing them, you'll continue to have the same results. For example, if you constantly lose time by checking social media or going online while at work, the solution isn't to buy a day planner to keep you focused because it doesn't address your habit. The result is you've spent money on a day planner and still lose time by going online or checking social media. The solution is to remove the app while at work or find a challenging project to work on. You don't always have to develop a new set of habits. Improving your existing habits is just as important in achieving your goals.

The second way to recognize your habits is to pay attention to what you repeatedly do in *familiar* situations. Habits do not suddenly appear. You're closely acquainted with them. What you want to pay attention to are the frequent moments in which they arise. When in a familiar situation, what do you habitually do?

Here are some examples:

- In meetings, do you interrupt others?
- When a leadership role becomes available, do you promote people only within your peer network?
- Do you tend to promote extroverts for leadership positions?
- When in a room with leaders, do you doubt yourself and have negative self-talk?

By paying attention to the moments when your habits arise, you can become self-aware of them. You can also become aware of your habits by noticing when you're inclined to begin your habitual pattern or response. All habits begin when you have the inclination to do something. By being self-aware of your habits and knowing that you *want* to gain this self-knowledge, you can approach your day with a different outlook. What you look for, you will find.

Self-awareness of your habits must lead to self-improvement. Unlike James in our story, it's not enough to notice something *can* be improved and not do anything about it. You *must* make improvements if you want to ultimately improve. Paying attention to your habits can give you more control over what you do and want to do, giving you better direction over your day, career, and life as you recognize your habits and make any necessary changes. You can only improve what you're aware of. If you recognize what you habitually do, you can better control what you *want* to do.

Making Decisions About Your Habits

Once you're self-aware of your habits, it's time to make a decision about them. Do you want to keep the habits you're aware of or change them? Do you want to improve them? Are you happy and satisfied with what you repeatedly do? In popular books on habits, it's common to hear that habits are good, bad, and neutral. But technically, habits are *not* neutral. Habits always have an outcome, and they're done for a reason. Habits have a purpose. Some of your habits may be harmless, but that does not mean they're neutral. The habits you repeat are what you've chosen to do over another response. You, therefore, have a purpose in what you repeatedly do, as your habits have a predictable outcome. But having a purpose for a habit does not mean it's the best thing to do. It simply means it's a choice you repeatedly make. When self-aware of your habits, you observe that what you repeatedly do is what you've learned to do, and it's what you're *inclined* to repeat when the moment arises again. Your habits have an immediate outcome, which is what you're trying to achieve by repeating the action. Your habits can also have an ultimate outcome, which is the larger consequence or result of repeating them. For example, an immediate outcome of avoiding opportunities for growth is self-comfort, and the ultimate outcome is a loss of career opportunities by staying within your comfort zone. An immediate outcome to mindlessly scrolling on your phone is entertainment, and the ultimate outcome is wasted time. An immediate outcome of taking credit for someone else's work is a feeling of importance, and the ultimate outcome is a loss of trust from your peers. An immediate outcome of addiction is pleasure, and the ultimate outcome is mental or physical harm and ruined relationships.

Once you become self-aware of your habits, I encourage you to go through the following suggested questions to help you make a decision about them. Take your time with each question and reflect on what it means to you.

- **Does my habit help me achieve my ultimate goal?** This question helps remind you of your most important goals and values and if what you habitually do aligns with them. If you're a leader and your goal is to motivate your team, then multitasking and not listening when they talk to you always leads to the same result: an unmotivated team that feels unimportant and ignored. Your habit of multitasking when you should be listening hinders your goal of motivating your team.

- **Does my habit reflect the truth of reality?** Is what you habitually think or do true? You can habitually think or do something because of false beliefs. This often happens when you habitually believe or do something because you were taught to do it by others, or you do something habitually in response to others. For example, you can falsely believe something negative about yourself or others because you were taught those negative things, but by truly examining your life or interacting with what you were taught to fear, you realize that the information you believed was wrong.

■ **Is this a good habit?** This is the most basic question to ask and encourages you to consider the outcome for yourself and others. Your habits have an outcome; they lead to something. The question helps you think about the end result but also what you do to achieve that end result. It's wrong to assume that only the outcome of your habits matters. What you do to achieve that outcome is also important. A habit can give you satisfaction (outcome), but what you do (action) to achieve that satisfaction can be wrong. You must think about what you repeatedly do and not just the outcome of what you do.

For example, an office manager in a medical office can habitually believe that profit is the most important thing. To achieve this goal, the office manager habitually overloads the medical providers in the office with patients and cuts safety procedures to save money. The end result is higher profits but also no rest periods for the team, short conversations with patients, a decrease in patient diagnostic information, an increase in diagnostic errors due to fatigue, mistakes in treatment plans, staff burnout, and turnover. The office manager prefers profit over people. The end results don't always support what you do to get them—the ends don't always justify the means.

- **Is this the best way, or is there a better way?** How can this be improved? How do I make this better? This question should be applied to *anything* you frequently do during the week. For any recurring activities, ask yourself how can they be improved. For example, when you begin your workday and automatically start your work routines, ask yourself, "Is this the best way, or is there a better way?" There are things you automatically repeat without thinking about it. You're accustomed to doing them. It is in these moments where improvement can happen. It takes time and attention, but by paying attention to what you repeatedly do and making improvements, significant growth can happen. Sometimes you can be so comfortable repeating an action or behavior that you don't focus on improving what you repeatedly do. You can be frustrated with the results or believe your results are the best you can do without ever realizing that an improvement in what you repeatedly do can lead to a positive change in results. There are tasks you frequently do that are routine. When you're about to start a repeated task or activity, you're inclined to do it in the same way as before. In these moments, pause to ask yourself if what you're about to do is the best way or if there's a better way.

If you find it difficult to remember the questions, it's sufficient to only remember, "Is my habit something that's good to do?" The question will prompt you to think about whether your habit is good for you, good for the people you care about, good for achieving your goals, or if there's a better way. The question also reminds you of your most important values and whether what you repeatedly do aligns with your values. Recognizing your habits is the first step to achieving the outcome you desire, and the second step is making a decision about them. You'll begin to notice your habits only if you want to notice them. But when you do, it can be an opportunity for improvement.

Be Curious About Yourself

You've learned to pay attention to what you habitually do and make decisions on what you want to do, and you understand the process of becoming better in all areas of life is a lifelong journey. The opportunity to keep learning and improving is what brings energy, enthusiasm, and excitement to each day. To improve and take responsibility for your habits, develop a curiosity and drive to learn about yourself. It is important to have the right outlook. Every day is an opportunity to learn and get better. That should be your daily attitude. You should not avoid, ignore, or give up on your habits. You're choosing to pay attention to what you habitually think and do to improve what you think and do. You may become uncomfortable with what you observe and learn, but it's through these moments that you realize you can overcome more than you think you can.

What are the thoughts and actions you habitually repeat at work, in a group environment, or in response to familiar moments? What have you taught yourself to repeatedly think and do? What have you learned and been conditioned by others to believe and do? It's in your response to a familiar moment that you become most aware of your habits. The following are a few examples of common habits.

- Dwelling on the things you don't have but others do
- Criticizing others
- Negative self-talk
- Fear of trying something new
- Quickly diminishing compliments you receive
- Focusing on everything that's wrong with your life
- Not appreciating the good things in your life
- Excessively talking about your achievements
- Using the same agenda for every meeting
- Not writing things down and subsequently forgetting what you wanted to remember
- Believing you have to lead or open every meeting
- Believing you have to attend every meeting, conference call, or video conference
- Constantly checking your inbox even when you don't have a new notification
- Believe something is wrong if every hour of your work calendar isn't full
- Feeling guilty about having free time or taking a vacation
- Always saying yes to requests
- Always saying no to requests
- Interrupting people when they're speaking
- Repeating the same vague catchphrases in meetings
- Managing your inbox/calendar in the same way

- Feeling bad about yourself when others do well
- Minimizing other people's success
- Believing you don't deserve or are not good enough for a promotion
- Constantly worrying about what other people think of you
- Being easily distracted
- Overspending and not saving money
- Procrastinating

It's sufficient to become aware of your habits without immediately trying to understand what causes you to think and behave in repetitive ways. The causes of your habits are not as important as becoming self-aware of them and then making a decision to keep or change them. It's important to remember that not all your habits are bad. Some have been useful to you, and many reflect your good qualities and have led you to success. Some of your habits are a recognition of what you do well, and others can be improved upon to further your goals. You can achieve greater success by taking responsibility for your habits.

Be Curious About What You Accept and Repeat from Others

We have learned that the first goal of self-awareness is noticing your habits, and the second is making a decision about them. In achieving your first goal, you also become aware of what you've learned and acquired from others. You become aware of the ideas you accept from others that influence your habits. It's easy to repeat the thoughts and actions of others, especially when belonging to a group environment.

Yawning, for example, is something people automatically repeat when observing others who yawn. We can similarly repeat the habits of others by observing them. All habits are a form of repetition, and the more you repeat one-time decisions or responses, the more habitual the actions become.

To notice your habits in a group environment, become aware of when you feel *inclined* to repeat the thoughts and actions of others, as well as when you *are* repeating the thoughts and actions of others. You want to become self-aware of your habits and then make a conscious decision instead of repeating what others say and do automatically. Part of this is paying attention to your group environment and knowing that you are receiving ideas that influences your thoughts, beliefs, and habits. You're always in a learning environment.

How do you know when you're accepting an idea? There are two ways to know. First, *be present* with your thoughts when in a group setting. If you've ever said to yourself, "That's a great idea!" then you have experienced being present with an idea. Being present with your thoughts requires a learning attitude. You must *want* to notice your thoughts when in a group setting. You *can* notice when you are inclined to accept or repeat something from others. Your thoughts are constantly interacting with the words and actions of the people around you.

For example, if you're listening to a political commentator on the news or on social media, your thoughts are *receiving* information, and you're quickly making decisions about it. When you notice you're *inclined* to accept or repeat an idea that's being presented to you, you can mentally pause and say to yourself, "Let me think about what they just said." This gives you the mental space to think about what you're receiving. You can further ask yourself, "Is what they're saying true?" or, "How can I verify what they said?" This gives you enough distance from what's presented to you to think about what you want to accept and repeat. This same thinking process can be applied any time you're in a group environment or when listening to the ideas of others.

Saying the phrase, "Let me think about this," is simply a reminder that you're *able* to consciously consider the ideas and information presented to you within a group environment *before* accepting or repeating it. There's a mental space between listening and accepting.

Here are more catchphrases that are repeated within meetings that catch on quickly. The examples show how easy it is to repeat what you hear within your group environment. What you repeat, you accept for that moment. I've included the meaning next to the catchphrases. See if you can catch yourself repeating these phrases (or any other phrases) next time in a meeting:

- "This is a sausage-making meeting" – a meeting or an activity that's still developing
- "We need to build our muscle" – strengthen or use a skill
- "We need more cover fire" – the need for more information or an overview
- "We need more air support" – people to provide specific support
- "We need to all be on the same sheet of music" – knowledge of the same strategy
- "We need to march to the same drummer or drumbeat" – having the same strategy

- "What's our cadence?" – the timing or frequency of an event or activity
- "Can we do a double click?" – a second review
- "Let me get a pulse check" – review if the audience understands or has any questions
- "Let's do a deep dive" – a further, detailed review
- "They're a warm prospect" – a person who knows who you are
- "They're a cold prospect" – a person who doesn't know who you are
- "Let's get granular" – more detailed and specific
- "This is an a-ha moment" – a moment of insight
- "We need to stand shoulder-to-shoulder" – work closely with the employees
- "Can you give me a 30,000 feet view?" – a general overview of information
- "What's our why? How do we find our why?" – the primary or motivating reason
- "We need to do some hand-to-hand combat" – get technical and specific
- "This is an end-to-end process" – a thorough process
- "It's a check-the-box activity" – a routine done with little attention
- "We need a paradigm shift" – a different way of thinking
- "We need to pivot" – to change direction

We've learned the first way to notice what you're accepting or repeating in a group environment is to be present. The second way is to notice *how you feel*. Instead of "catching" your thoughts, you want to "catch" your emotions, as your emotions are good in-dicators of what's on your mind. Your thoughts are so quick that you can be unaware of them. But how you feel is something you *can* be aware of. It's hard not to notice if you're feeling a certain way. When you have an idea, and you say to yourself, "That's a great idea!" you *also* have an accompanying feeling, such as mo-tivation or excitement. When you disagree, you have displeasure. Your feelings rise to a conscious level you can observe, similar to a sunrise. Your feelings and thoughts are indicators you're interacting with your environment.

Sometimes you can become so enthusiastic that you forget to think. When people say, "My emotions got the best of me," they mean their emotions led and controlled their actions. You *can* be prodded to think and feel a certain way when others intention-ally seek to manipulate your emotions. When someone brings up a topic or view that creates a strong emotional response from you, it's a way to influence you to think or respond in a specific way. In moments of hysteria, you accept or repeat the ideas and actions of others without thinking about them. You can become hypnotized by moments of enthusiasm, fear, and anger. By no-ticing how you feel, you can become aware and take control of your thoughts. It's easier to identify when you disagree with others than when you agree and accept their ideas. This is why it's important to be vigilant when hearing ideas and information from others. You may accept and repeat them without being conscious of it.

Sometimes it's only by noticing what you repeat from oth-ers that you realize you've accepted something from the people within your surroundings. As a child growing up in Los Angeles,

I closely followed the Los Angeles Dodgers. When I watched the Dodgers on television or my other favorite Major League Baseball (MLB) players, I would mimic their swings as they stood to bat or mimic their pitching windup as they pitched. When a batter was up to bat, I picked up my bat and swung. When a pitcher was up to pitch, I would drop my bat and pick up my glove and baseball. As they swung, I swung; as they pitched, I pitched. To this day, I still do a pitching windup in the kitchen and living room, and my wife continues to roll her eyes and say, "Keep dreaming."

When I played Little League baseball, the topics of discussion among my teammates were the swings of the MLB players who hit many home runs and the pitches of the MLB pitchers that were "nasty" to hit (challenging to hit). We emulated the MLB players. We bought their shoes, wore their jerseys, chewed their gum, and copied their habits. During batting practice, we would replicate the swings of the home-run hitters. We wanted to replicate their "power swings." During pitching practice, we would attempt the "nasty" pitches of the great pitchers. We wanted a strong arm, and we wanted strikeouts.

When not mimicking our idols, we had our own natural swings, and we had our own natural pitching windups that were different from our heroes. We became better hitters and better pitchers when we worked on our *own* natural styles while still using the techniques of those we idolized, and conversely, we were worse hitters and pitchers when we copied those we admired. In time, we each discovered we could hit home runs with our own swings, and we could strike out batters with our own pitching style. If we wanted to improve a particular aspect of our performance, we could study our idols for tips on how they held their hands, how they balanced their feet, or where their eye coordination was, but we did not have to replicate them. We did not have more home runs by copying their swings, and we did not have more strikeouts by pitching like them. We did not have better results by copying our idols. We had better results by improving upon what we learned.

Professional sports players are good at what they do, and they continually improve upon their talents by learning from themselves and learning from others. They take responsibility for working toward what they want to achieve. If they want to perform better, they identify what they want to improve and take responsibility for working toward it. But if every current professional athlete simply repeated and copied their idols, they would never have developed their own talents to become professional sports players. At a certain point in their development, every professional athlete becomes their own player. Great players are great in their own way. Great leaders are great in their own way as well.

Self-awareness helps you become aware of what you accept and repeat from your group environment. Self-awareness of what you repeat from others helps realign your thoughts and actions toward your values. If you find yourself thinking, saying, or doing something based on the influence of others, and if that is not a part of your values, you can realign and recenter yourself around your most important values. Self-awareness helps to re-center you to be the person you truly want to be.

Choose What You Want for Yourself

To take responsibility for your habits is to take responsibility for your future. If you choose to continue doing the same thing or responding in the same habitual way, that's how you will *continue* to respond and have the same outcome. Nothing changes unless something changes. Self-awareness, whether it leads you to maintain your habits or if it gives you the resolution to change direction, helps you take greater responsibility for yourself and the future you desire. Self-awareness leads you to that moment of saying, "This is what I want for myself." If you want more control over your future, you must have greater control over your actions. Since habits are what you repeatedly do, then becoming self-aware of them and taking responsibility for what you *want* to do is a step in achieving the future you desire.

Self-awareness of your habits is the goal of this book. Are you aware of what you habitually do and aware of the outcome? Are you aware of what's important to you? Pause your reading, and ask yourself, "What do I want for *myself*?"

By paying attention to your habits and taking responsibility for them, you can improve the achievement of your goals and the direction of your life. You can become better at anything by paying attention to what you habitually do, then making a decision on what you want to do. Only you can make the decision to improve.

Where are your habitual beliefs, thoughts, and actions leading you? Are your habits helping you achieve your goals? Are they helping you achieve what's important to you? Are your habits what you *want* to do? Do your habits of thought reflect the truth of reality? Self-awareness helps you make a decision about what you want for yourself. The power to choose is the power to ask questions and to make a decision. The power to choose is the power to determine your direction. The power to choose is to realize you're not powerless.

Self-awareness is the power to ask yourself, "Why? Why do I habitually repeat the same thoughts and actions in familiar moments? Why do I keep responding in the same way? Why do I keep doing the same thing? Why do I repeat the same ideas, beliefs, and activities within my group environment? Why *should I* continue in my repetition? Why *should I* continue believing thoughts and ideas that are false? Why *should* I continue doing actions that are not good for me? Why not start a new direction today?"

When you're self-aware of your habits, you're thinking about what you want to accept. You're thinking about what is good for you. You're reevaluating your habits. Self-awareness leads to taking greater responsibility for what you habitually do, and for what you *want* to do. You're responsible for working *toward* achieving what you want for yourself. It does not matter if your habits were acquired from repetition or from your group environment. You may not have had a choice in the habits you've developed because of the ideas presented to you, which you believed. But you *can* choose what you want to accept, repeat, and continue. You can manage yourself to improve and achieve greater success by taking responsibility for your habits. By doing so, you will have more control over what you want to do and the results you want to see.

Managing yourself is successfully managing yourself into the future. Managing yourself today leads to a better tomorrow as you start becoming the person you want to be. You repeat the habits you *want* to repeat. There is freedom in being the person you want to be. Your habits are not *who* you are. Your habits are *what* you repeatedly do in familiar moments, and you can change the pattern once you become aware of what you do. You are more than your habits.

In leadership, your few decisions matter greatly. It's important that you have the time to think about what you're doing and what you *want* to do. Be present with what you do, habitually do, and want to do. Pay attention to the present moment. By paying attention to what you do, you can improve the achievement of your goals and the direction of your life. You can have more control over what you do and want to do. You can have more control over what's important to you. Managing your habits for success helps you become the person you truly want to be.

Notes

Notes

PART

II

DEVELOPING NEW HABITS

By now, you've learned to pay greater attention to yourself and your environment. You've learned to become self-aware of your habits, and you've started making the decision to improve the habits that need to change. You've learned to recognize and accept the ideas of your group environment that are true to reality, good for you and others, and help you become a better person and leader. The first part of the book focused on how to become self-aware of your habits and how to make the decision to improve them. The second part of the book and final chapter focus on how to develop *new* habits.

The style of this part of the book is different from the first part of the book. The principles to learn are written in a step-by-step instructional format that is easy to review and repeat. Developing new habits is a learning process, and you must constantly repeat the principles. As you've learned, habits are a repetition of what you do, and learning is a repetition of what to do.

CHAPTER 5

HOW TO DEVELOP NEW HABITS

C hanging your habits and developing new habits are different things. To begin a new habit does not always require you to change your old habits, but to change your habits, you do need to develop new habits. Whether you want to start something new that you've never done before or start something new because you're tired of what you repeatedly do, you *can* begin new habits.

1) Do What's Important to You.

The most important thing in developing a new habit is *wanting* it. You must want and have the desire for something new or different. What you desire to do must be important to you. What's important to you may be different from what's important to others.

The habits that bring others success or status may be desirable, but that does not mean it's also desirable for *you*.

In developing new habits, honesty is important. You must be self-aware and honest with the habits you want to change, and you must be honest with the reasons why you want to pursue a new habit.

Doing something that is important to *you* is the beginning of all achievements.

2) Set Goals.

To do anything different from what you repeatedly do and to achieve something new, you must determine what you want to do. Select the goals you want to achieve and be as specific as possible. When you have a goal, you have a purpose for what you do, and when you have a purpose, you pursue it because it's important. In setting your goals, you're asking yourself, "What's important to *me*?" Write down the most important goals you want to achieve in the next six to twelve months You can write them below or in the notes section at the end of this chapter:

- I want to...
- I want to...
- I want to...

Sometimes you can have the desire to change or want something new but without any clarity on what you want to achieve or pursue. You have a restless desire without direction. If you can determine the goals you want to achieve, and if that goal is important to you, your habits will begin to take shape. Your habits follow your purpose.

For example, when writing this book, I did not set out to have the habit of writing every morning at dawn. I wrote every morning because I felt an overwhelming desire to pursue it. My passion for pursuing the project led to the discipline of writing every morning. This book was written solely through passion and persistence. The habit of writing daily followed my goal, and yet it was only because of writing daily that the goal was achieved.

When setting your goals, select an ultimate goal that gives you the motivation to pursue your more short-term goals. What's the ultimate purpose of your goal? For example, if you have the bad habit of overspending money and you want the habit of *saving money*, then saving money is your goal. But saving money is not specific enough because it's not the ultimate reason why you should save money. If your reason for saving money is to have enough money to *travel* every year because traveling is important to you, then you've uncovered your ultimate goal, which is tied to what's important to you. Therefore, you want to change your habit of overspending money because you want to have money for what's important to you—traveling. You want to travel more often, and to do that, you'll need to save more money. Your habit of saving money becomes more important than your habit of overspending it.

After setting your goals, you must also know what *to do* to achieve them. This is to ask yourself, "How?" and "What do I do?" In the example above, if your goal is to save more money, *how* will you do it? *What* will you do to save more money? Suggested answers include:

- automatically saving a portion of your income (paying yourself first)
- tracking your fixed and discretionary spending
- budgeting
- planning your weekly meals
- reviewing your fixed expenses every six months to determine whether lower prices are available
- reducing your credit cards to only one or two
- reducing your online subscriptions to only what's most important to you

As a second example, let's say you want to change your habit of *interrupting* others when speaking. When you catch yourself inclined to interrupt others or when you do interrupt others when speaking, you can do the following:

- apologize and wait your turn
- write down what you want to say
- think about what you want to say instead of saying it immediately
- listen to what others have to say first
- ask others to remind you when you're interrupting them

A change in your habits is a change in how you respond to a familiar moment. You change your response by planning a different response. You must know what response to have; in other words, you must know what to do differently.

It is easier to achieve your goals when they're aligned with your values. Your values make your commitment to achieving your goals stronger. Knowing what's important to you also helps prioritize your goals. A common problem in achieving something is the attempt to achieve too many things and losing focus. Whatever habit you're trying to build is best achieved when it's both your goal and aligns with your values.

For example, if you want to be consistent with exercising (goal), then you will exercise more frequently if health (value) is what's important to you. Valuing your health supports the formation of other habits such as eating well, sleeping well, feeling optimistic, being productive, and avoiding harmful substances.

If you have a habit you'd like to achieve, and it's not supported by your values, then you will not remain consistent with your habit. If waking up at 5:00 a.m. is your goal, you can achieve it by waking up at 5:00 a.m. But what happens after you wake up? What do you start doing? If you begin to aimlessly scroll on your phone, and that's a habit you want to change, you've awoken at 5:00 a.m. just to continue a bad habit. But if waking up at 5:00 a.m. leads you to exercise, write, meditate, or appreciate the day, then you've aligned it to something positive.

Your goal *leads* to fulfilling what's most important to you— your values. Your goals, values and habits should support each other. Habits are simply what you repeat, but it's your goals and values that give them direction. Your habits will follow what's important to you.

3) Create a Supportive Environment.

In the world of team sports, there's a performance advantage the home team receives, known as home-field advantage. When a team plays at their home field, they become more confident of winning. The environment supports a team's ability and confidence to win through the encouragement they receive from the audience, the availability of resources each player needs to support their routines, and the removal of distractions that hinder performance. A supportive environment makes it easier to succeed.

To make it easier to develop and remain consistent with new habits, create a supportive environment. This is to ask yourself, "What environment or culture will help me best achieve my habits?" You are *creating* an environment to succeed. The same attention you place when following a dinner recipe is the same level of attention needed to create the outcome you desire. You can find or create a supportive environment. Creating a supportive environment is important but not as important as having a clear goal, desire, or purpose for what you want to achieve. Passion is important. You can wear expensive, name-brand exercise clothes, have high-end workout machines, and buy the healthiest food, but without the internal desire to exercise, the outerwear will not get you moving. But with a strong desire, you *will* exercise despite not having any of the resources mentioned. An environment *supports* your goals; it does not achieve your goals. Here are some suggestions to help you create an environment of success.

Join or form a group.

Belonging to a group that shares the same interests will help you develop, maintain, and improve your positive habits. If you want to develop the habit of walking outside, exercising, reading, writing, journaling, improving at your profession, or improving at your hobbies, such as golf or anything else, then joining with others on the same journey will keep you consistent. You'll learn good ideas and have motivating examples to help you on your journey.

Set reminders.

Reminders keep you focused on what's important and what's needed to achieve your outcome. Reminders are like having your own personal coach in whatever habit you want to develop or improve. Reminders to do something can be as easy as writing down your tasks on a *to-do* list or checklist, setting up reminders on your calendar, or setting up physical reminders in the areas you frequently visit.

For example, an area you frequently visit is the refrigerator within your home. We place pictures, magnets, certificates, quotes, and to-do lists on our refrigerators, and they serve as reminders. If it's trash day in your neighborhood, and you forget to take out the trash, you'll be reminded it's trash day by hearing the distinct sound of the garbage truck and by noticing that all your neighbors have put out their trash bins to be picked up.

An important thing to remember about reminders is they don't do the work for you, and they can't force you to do something you don't want to do. This goes back to our first principle of only starting the habits that are important to you. Reminders help keep you focused, disciplined, and consistent with only the things you *want* to do. Your habits take time to change, and reminders help change your habits one repetition at a time.

Prepare for success.

Success at anything requires action. You must *do* something to achieve your outcome. To develop new habits, you must prepare to achieve them by focusing on the parts that lead to success. Preparation is important. When going on vacation or taking a trip, you prepare to fly by buying a plane ticket, selecting the best time and airport, the transportation to and from your destination, the clothes you will wear, and the places you will visit. After your trip, people tend to ask you, "How was your trip?" The focus is on the experience and the outcome, but they both depend on you preparing to have a good trip.

What are the smaller activities that help what you want to achieve? For example, if your goal is to develop the habit of exercising daily, then list the parts that will lead you to achieve it:

- Your workout clothes need to be clean and available (and not lost somewhere in your laundry).
- You need to select the best time to exercise.
- You should know what exercises to do when you start exercising.

- You need to sleep enough hours to have the energy and stamina to exercise.
- You need to track your progress.

Habits are not one big thing but the product of smaller things coming together. You must prepare and expect to succeed.

Celebrate!

In developing new habits, the smallest achievement should be celebrated. When you begin doing what you want to do, it's an achievement, no matter how small it is. The feeling of success when crossing something off your to-do list is what you want to experience. You've done something you did not do before, and that is something to recognize and celebrate!

To create greater psychological momentum and repeat what you want to do, write down the day, the moment, and how you felt. You can forget these important moments, and writing them down makes them historical. They are milestones to remember. The message here is that since you did it once, you *can* do it again. As you write down every moment when you repeat the habit you want, you are forming a list of achievements. No matter how small the moment of success, write it down and indicate how you felt. This will build your confidence and give you positive thoughts that will dispel any negative thinking or frustration you may develop during the moments when you doubt yourself, regress to your old habits, or skip the repetition of your habit. When needing a confidence boost, look back at your list. It's a factual record of what you have done and *can* do again. By celebrating your achievements, no matter how small, you will develop pride and confidence in what you've done and in yourself. This will help you believe in your potential.

Working with a Challenging Environment.

In creating a supportive environment, you're creating a culture to support your success. But sometimes, you're limited with what you can do in creating a supportive environment. You can change aspects of your environment, but you may be unable to completely change your environment. In these moments, find the most essential activities you can control to support your habits and begin to train yourself to be less responsive to your environment. You can train yourself to be less responsive by knowing what triggers you habitually respond to and planning a different response. For example, if you're in a busy workplace environment with distractions and tasks that compete with your time, you're unable to change this environment, but you can take productive steps to control what you want to repeat. You know the distractions, and you know what you can control to become less distracted and more focused. Think about the essential activities you can control to support your habits.

One of the habits you likely want to acquire is the habit of being productive with your time. Productivity is the ability to accomplish things and the effective use of available time. How do you control your productivity within a workplace environment that is distracting? One suggestion is to use a to-do list that you control. By writing down what you need to accomplish, you don't waste time figuring out what to do; instead, when the available time arises to act, you act immediately with what you've planned to do. This goes back to the importance of preparing to succeed. You may be able to only accomplish one task out of your ten tasks for the day, but in an environment that works against you, achieving one task is an accomplishment and the best of what you can do. Any progress *is* progress.

Writers, for instance, can incorrectly believe that inspiration and a block of time are needed to write. Writers can endlessly search for the perfect time and environment to write. Inspiration and blocks of time do help, but if you're inspired and don't have the blocks of time, does that prevent you from writing? You may not have a large portion of your day to write, but you do have smaller portions of time throughout the day where you *can* write. The smaller portions add up to following through on your habit of writing.

You can also train yourself to be less responsive to the triggers of people, situations, and things in your environment that cause you to habitually respond in a certain way. You can predict your habits because you know how you respond to the familiar moments when your habits arise. You know when you're inclined to respond in a habitual way. Your habits are a movie that you've watched over and over again. You know how it begins and ends. You know the major characters involved. When you notice your habits arising, you can:

- Remind yourself it's a learned behavior
- Remind yourself you can choose to do something different

- Respond in a different way
- Complete the habit and not be too hard on yourself

To respond in a different way, you must first think about alternative ways to respond. Without knowing a different way, you'll repeat the same way. There are two things you can do. First, work on understanding and changing your thoughts about the situation or moment that triggers your habitual response. You respond in a particular way because of what you believe about the situation or moment that triggers your response. You can change how you perceive the situation or moment, which helps begin to change how you habitually respond to the moment.

If you habitually respond with anger toward someone, for example, you do so because of what you believe or know about the person. You can change how you perceive the person while still being true to what you know. By changing how you perceive someone, you change your response.

You've done the first step of work on understanding and changing your thoughts about the situation or moment that triggers your habitual response. Second, work on your habitual response. It is hard to quickly change an ingrained response you're comfortable repeating, but change does happen slowly. Pay attention to what you habitually do and interrupt it by introducing a new response. When you become habitually angry at someone, introduce these practices:

- Slow deep breathing
- Mental repetition of positive thinking, phrases, and reminders

- Looking elsewhere to change your focus
- Taking a walk

Anger is a powerful emotion brought on by pain, being hurt by someone, or having an inability to control a situation or someone. You can change your thoughts about the situation that causes you anger by understanding the reason behind your anger (step 1) and by taking active steps to change your habitual response (step 2).

By continually practicing your new response when the habitual response arises, the power of the habitual response begins to weaken. It's quite possible you may never completely remove your habitual response, but you can minimize it to the point where you can quickly move away from it.

4) Be Patient and Have a Learning Attitude.

Change takes time. You've learned or have been taught to repeatedly do something in particular moments. You repeat your habits because they achieve an outcome. You have habits for a reason. You can become frustrated that you can't change your habits. However, your frustration is a positive sign that you've grown tired of what you repeatedly do. You're aware of what you do and want something different. You want something better. This awareness is a significant milestone in your desire to improve and become better. Frustration is a good sign that you want to improve.

Changing your habits requires a change in your perspective. You're changing your habits by learning to do something different. You're learning something new to then do it. When you have a profession or an occupation, you learn the knowledge and skills of that job and apply what you learn. Over time you get better at what you do as long as you continue to learn and improve what you do. You get better at your job because you focus on it daily. The learning process of your profession is no different from learning new habits. You've learned to do something one way, and now you're learning to do it a different way.

Habits are meant to be repeated, but that does not mean they have to be repeated in perfect sequence. There's no need to become frustrated and disappointed if you don't perfectly repeat your habits. Contrary to popular belief, missing two moments of repetition is not the beginning of a failed habit. What matters most with the success of your habits is consistency—repeating your habits over time. Repeating a habit in perfect sequence can lead to an undesirable outcome. You can exercise every day for a month, but too much exertion will lead to injuries and inadequate rest periods, which is when your muscles grow. Missed opportunities to repeat your habits are opportunities to achieve a better perspective on what you've committed yourself to doing. Taking a day, two days, or a week off from exercising can lead to better growth by achieving the necessary rest periods and by reevaluating your workout plan. Missing a day (or two) from repeating your habit can give you greater energy, motivation, and perspective when returning to your habit.

It is not how frequently you repeat your habits, but that when they are repeated, they are truthful to reality, align with your goals and values, and are good to continue repeating. It's the *quality* of the habit rather than the *frequency* of repetition. It's not how often you repeat something but that what's repeated is what you want to do and is the best thing to do. Life continues to change, people change, and situations change. Your habits must also adapt to change and the outcome you want. If being on a specific diet doesn't give you the outcome you want, it's counterproductive to stay consistent with your diet. If a diet gives you the outcome you want, that doesn't mean you will never change your diet if there's a different diet that gives you a better outcome. What matters is your habits are what you want to do and are good to do.

You're learning to do something new, and you're *becoming* the person you want to be. Instead of focusing on what you're not doing or failing to do, focus on your progress. One positive repetition of what you want to do is a step in achieving it. For that moment, you *did* achieve it. And you can do it again.

Notes

Notes

ACKNOWLEDGMENTS

I would like to acknowledge the following people for their support of this book. I can't express my gratitude enough, but perhaps a scoop of my homemade gelato is a start.

Thank you to my wife for her support, patience, and understanding during all the long hours and moments I said, "Just a little longer. I'll be done in a minute." This book would not be possible without her. I owe you a new pair of shoes.

Thank you to my editor, Beth Lottig, for her wisdom, creativity, vision, and organizational abilities. She's the magic behind this book.

Thank you to Managing Director Jeanne Sun of JPMorgan Chase. Her reader's feedback was valuable in the improvement of the book.

And lastly, thank you, dear reader, for your interest in this book. You are the motivation for its existence.

ABOUT THE AUTHOR

Danny Zelaya is an executive director at a Fortune 500 bank and a chaplain in the California Army National Guard. He began his professional career out of seminary school as a youth pastor. He later became a financial advisor with Merrill Lynch and after four years, moved into management and leadership. His writing interests include business management and leadership, personal development, and Christian meditations. He lives outside of Los Angeles with his family and is a lifelong Dodgers fan (*go Dodger blue!*). You can catch him on Instagram and Facebook making new weekly dinner recipes for his family. Sometimes he's successful.

What did you like about this book? What other types of personal development books do you want to read? You can email the author at the following address: managingyourhabits@gmail.com

You can also follow the author on these social platforms:

Instagram: zelaya_d
Facebook: Danny Zelaya
LinkedIn: Danny Zelaya

If this book can make a difference in someone's life, please share it with them.

www.ingramcontent.com/pod-product-compliance
Lightning Source LLC
Chambersburg PA
CBHW060322130626
46553CB00003B/886